Prac Guide to Florida Retirement

Betty McGarry

Pineapple Press, Inc.
Sarasota, Florida

For Bessie,
whose life was short and bitter, but
whose dreams were long and sweet.

Inquiries should be addressed to Pineapple Press, Inc. P.O. Drawer 16008, Sarasota, Florida 34239

Library of Congress Cataloging-in-Publication Data

McGarry, Betty, 1917-
    A practical guide to Florida retirement / by Betty
      McGarry.—1st ed.
      p. cm.
    Bibliography: p.
    Includes index.
    ISBN 0-910923-61-2 : $8.95
    1. Retirement, Places of—Florida. I. Title.
HQ1063.M42   1989   88-31220
646.7′9—dc19   CIP

1st Edition
  10 9 8 7 6 5 4 3 2 1

Composition by Hillsboro Printing, Tampa, Florida
Printed and bound by Cushing-Malloy, Inc., Ann Arbor, Michigan

CONTENTS

ACKNOWLEDGMENTS

The author is grateful to the Florida Department of Commerce, Division of Tourism, for most of the illustrations in this book. All those not otherwise credited were provided from the photo library of the Division.

She also wishes to thank the staff of the Cooper Memorial Library of Clermont for its patient help. Portions of the text were verified by friends with expertise, particularly Denton Cook and John Reynolds. Requests for information from other departments of the state and from a number of businesses were promptly and courteously answered. Last, she is most appreciative of the invaluable advice and support given by editor June Cussen.

1. Your Place in the Sun

Welcome to Florida!

The day you arrived in your new home state, 2,400 other newcomers crossed the borders in search of their private utopias. The same day 1,400 moved out, making a net gain of 1,000 new residents a day. *Every day.*

In 1900 Florida was 33rd among the states in population. Early in 1988 it became the fourth most populous state in the country, following California, New York, and Texas and displacing Pennsylvania. During those 88 years the total population of the United States tripled while the population of Florida multiplied by a factor of eighteen!

What brings all these new residents to what is really a mid-sized state?

There are many reasons, of course, but a few of these are the most common. A portion follow their employers who have moved to the Sunbelt. Others are looking for work in a growing area. Some relocate to be with family and friends. Many want to escape the rigors of Northern winters. And then there are those, like you, who want to pursue the dream of retirement in the mecca of the South.

Besides age, you probably have a lot in common with the other retirees. Chances are you came from the Northeast or the Midwest. You've been to Florida before as a visitor. You'd like a small, comfortable, easy-to-care-for home. You're eager to pursue the hobbies and interests you never had enough time for before. You're pleased to be getting away from the snow and the cold. Probably you have friends already here, and possibly you still have a house "back home" where you will go to avoid the humidity of Florida's summers.

In spite of the advice of friends and the visits you've made to the state before you retired, you still have a lot to learn about your new home. If the glossy pictures in the tourist brochures

The Six regions of Florida

and the materials given out by the chambers of commerce don't tell you enough, or seem too good to be true, perhaps you'll be willing to trust this guide, written by a resident who came before, to help you learn what to expect and what mistakes to avoid in living with the important decision you have made. There are indeed errors the uninformed can make that will cost time and money and cause unhappiness, and there are pleasant surprises, too, in the good life of your future.

For convenience, the state has been divided into six regions, according to the sections shown on the official map of the Division of Tourism, a copy of which you no doubt received at the welcome center on some visit to Florida. This division is mainly geographic, and within each region you'll find considerable diversity. No description of an area can hope to surpass a personal visit.

With that caution in mind, let's see the state where Summer spends the Winter.

1. Northwest (the Panhandle)

If you think you'll be nostalgic for familiar trees, gently rolling hills, and an occasional light snow that melts before you can say "shovel," you'll like the Northwest. It's the largest of the six regions, beginning at the border with Alabama on the west and

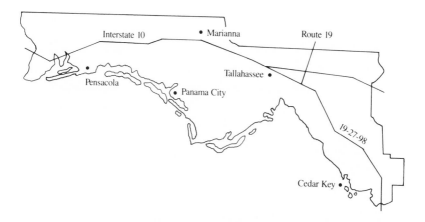

Northwest, the Panhandle

running to the Suwannee River about 230 miles to the east. It's also the most like the Old South. There are fewer people and more unspoiled land here than anywhere else in Florida except the Everglades. Even the cost of living touches the area more lightly than elsewhere in the state.

This is the area with long beaches noted for their white sands and good fishing. Here you will find two extensive state forests with camping and recreational facilities, Blackwater River and Apalachicola, and many wildlife preserves and museums of historical interest.

U.S. Interstate Highway 10 is the main east-west artery, but U.S. 98, running along the Gulf Coast and the offshore islands, is the scenic route. Along I-10 forests of pine cultivated for lumber, pulp, and by-products are interspersed with dairy farms. Hardwoods, especially several varieties of oak, encouraged by the sandy loam soil, cover the low hills. The third major highway is variously designated as U.S. 27, 19, or 48 depending on its destination. It joins the cities of the Panhandle to the Peninsula, and passes near the southernmost city in the region, Cedar Key. In that section of the highway the land changes character, trading rolling hills for tidal areas, undeveloped woodland, and farms.

The waters of the area offer great recreational opportunities from canoeing and sailing to swimming and surfing. Bays and coves expand the Intracoastal Waterway, which runs behind the barrier islands and through navigable rivers. Many rivers drain the region, including the two most important, the Apalachicola and the Suwannee. Natural springs, found in abundance, are sometimes features of state parks and sometimes developed into attractions by commercial interests, but in either case they're vital to the ecology and protected by state law.

Many of these naturally beautiful features are threatened by growth. The construction crane is replacing the mockingbird as the state symbol. This is most common in the coastal areas, where developers often build on land that should be left in its natural state. While new residents can't help adding to the growth, they can help by not compounding the problems it brings. Agencies fighting to save the natural resources are effective with public support, and enlightened voters can persuade legislators to protect the fragile environment.

Besides agricultural products and tourism, the economic health of the area is served by the presence of a number of military installations. The largest ones are the Pensacola Naval Air Station, home of the Blue Angel stunt fliers, and Eglin Air Force Base, which sprawls across three counties, ending at the beltway of Tallahassee.

The principal cities of the region provide varied amenities for their citizens. In Tallahassee, the capital, the state employs 31,000 workers, a third of the total work force in the metropolitan area. The state capitol complex, which includes an impressive 22-story executive office building, welcomes visitors. Florida State University and Florida Agricultural and Mechanical University are located here. Nearby are gardens and archaeological sites, state parks and wildlife refuges, and museums and historical markers. Wakulla Springs, a short trip south of the city, still retains the natural beauty of primitive Florida.

Pensacola, the westernmost city, lies in the Central Time Zone. It can lay claim to being the first settlement in the New World since the Spanish landed there in 1559. Unfortunately, the colony was short-lived, and the honor goes instead to St. Augustine, which in 1565 became the first permanent settlement in the New World. Pensacola is still proud of its heritage, preserved in three outstanding museums, a historical district, and a nearby Spanish fort. The University of West Florida, a branch of the statewide university system, has its campus here. The city has a zoo and botanical gardens and is the hub of 150 miles of islands and keys that stretch from Mississippi to the city of Destin.

The Fort Walton Beach/Destin area offers some of the greatest fishing in the state, attracting many anglers to its tournaments. The beaches are the main attraction. It's hard to believe, looking at the resort city Fort Walton has become, that as short

The 22-story "new" State Capitol Building in Tallahassee.

a time ago as 1940 the black bear population outnumbered the people. There are gardens in the city and an Indian Mound Museum, but dominating the hinterland is the largest military installation in the world, Eglin Air Force Base.

Panama City is a commercial port. It's best known for its amusements and water sports, but surrounding the glitter are wildlife preserves and state parks.

Marianna, located inland just off I-10, is a bustling town close to the only caverns in Florida. A visit to the Florida Caverns State Park can take you 65 feet below the surface. Contrast that with a hill in Walton County, halfway between Pensacola and Marianna near the Alabama border, that is the highest spot in Florida at 345 feet above sea level.

Cedar Key is a small town that once was a busy port. A hurricane in 1896 nearly wiped it out and destroyed for good its trade. Now it's a sleepy town and tourist attraction situated on one of the hundred islands called keys that lie offshore a few miles south of the mouth of the Suwannee River.

Average Fahrenheit temperatures and rainfall for representative cities of the region are:

City	January	July	Annual Precipitation
Tallahassee	53.9	81.3	56.86
Pensacola	54.1	81.8	63.69
Cedar Key	58.3	82.5	46.56

The principal newspapers with a net circulation (1987) of 50,000 or more are the *Pensacola News Journal* and the *Tallahassee Democrat*.

County	Population (1980 census)	Area (sq. mi.)	Density (pop./sq. mi.)
1. Bay	97,740	861(108)*	129.8
2. Calhoun	9,294	567	16.7
3. Dixie	7,751	709	11.3
4. Escambia	233,794	762(105)	355.9
5. Franklin	7,551	565	14.1
6. Gadsden	41,565	523	81.8
7. Gilchrist	5,767	348	17.0
8. Gulf	10,658	578	19.1

County	Population (1980 census)	Area (sq. mi.)	Density (pop./sq. mi.)
9. Hamilton	8,761	515	17.0
10. Holmes	14,723	484	31.8
11. Jackson	39,154	938	42.0
12. Jefferson	10,703	609	17.4
13. Lafayette	4,035	554	7.4
14. Leon	148,655	696	217.0
15. Levy	19,870	1,137	18.0
16. Liberty	4,260	845	5.1
17. Madison	14,894	708	21.2
18. Okaloosa	109,920	998(55)	116.4
19. Santa Rosa	55,988	1,152(128)	54.7
20. Suwannee	22,287	687	32.9
21. Taylor	16,532	1,052	16.0
22. Wakulla	10,887	635	17.7
23. Walton	21,300	1,135(89)	20.4
24. Washington	14,509	611	24.3

*indicates square miles of water included when the amount exceeds 50 sq. mi.
  (Source: *Florida Almanac*)

2. Northeast (Historic Region)
If you're excited by the ocean and like lots of people around you, the Northeast Coast may be your choice. If you want a quiet, rural life, the interior of this region is worth exploring.

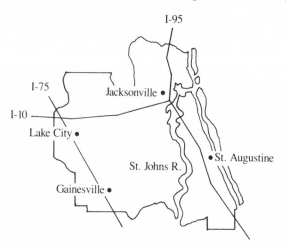

Northeast, the Historic Region

The earliest settlements in Florida began in this area, which is bounded roughly by the Georgia border, the Atlantic Ocean, the Suwannee River, and a line drawn westward from Ormond Beach to Gainesville. The state's major waterway, the St. Johns River, which flows into the ocean near Jacksonville, was a gateway taking early settlers into central Florida.

In contrast to the warm, often green-blue Gulf waters, the sea that washes the Atlantic beaches is cool and steel blue, and while the sands of the Northwest are white, those of the Northeast are golden. (One exception to the sand color occurs in the resort city of Amelia Island, which is proud of its white quartz beaches.)

Here are found the sea sports, the commercial attractions, the largest city in Florida, and urban sprawl, side by side with backwoods areas, nature preserves, and historical and cultural attractions.

The major roads in the region include a section of I-95, the interstate highway that runs unbroken from Maine to South Florida. I-10, which passes through the Panhandle, terminates its trip from the Far West in the city of Jacksonville. Along the coast runs State Highway A1A, which connects the barrier islands and should be a scenic route, but which, sadly, is lined with commercial establishments. Toward the western edge of the region I-75 enters Florida from the Midwest.

There are two national forests in this section: Osceola in Baker and Columbia Counties and a portion of Ocala National Forest in Putnam County.

Through the mouth of the St. Johns River passes the trade for the port of Jacksonville, the largest city in the state.

But outside the busy port and away from the river corridor are quiet rural areas that produce pine, food crops, and tobacco. In the arc around Duval County, you find scattered houses and small farms and few towns. North of Osceola Forest is the lower section of the Okefenokee Swamp, where there are alligators instead of people. Once outside the semicircle, the towns appear again, and along I-10 is Lake City, off I-75 is Gainesville, and at the south end of the region on the St. Johns River is Palatka.

Jacksonville claims it is the largest city in the world. Possibly it is in area, for the city boundaries are contiguous with those of Duval County. Because it's at the mouth of the St. Johns River, it was settled early and has historical sites from the Spanish Colonial, the Revolution, and the Civil War eras. Along with Miami, it is often the city used to represent Florida; for example, it was recently the host city for the display of the relics of King Tutankhamen. It has a beautiful civic center and the campus of the University of North Florida. Jacksonville Beach is its resort area, and a car ferry carries visitors to the nearby Mayport Naval Air Station.

St. Augustine's outstanding feature is its Old Town, a living museum of early Spanish rule. Among the many attractions is a museum that exhibits treasures from sunken Spanish ships. On the shore is the Castillo de San Marcos, a fort built to protect the city from the British. Every spring a dramatic presentation called "Cross and Sword" is given to depict the settlement of St. Augustine. There's a park in the Old Town where a visitor

Visitors can enjoy a carriage ride through the streets of "Old Town" St. Augustine.

can taste the strong-smelling mineral water that is purported to be from the fountain of youth that Ponce de Leon sought. A few miles south along the coast is Marineland, a center for the study of marine biology that also puts on an aquatic show for entertainment.

Lake City, like many Panhandle cities a place that prides itself on its conservatism, lies five miles east of the intersection of I-75 and I-10, in a pastoral setting next to the cypress swamps and wetlands of the 150,000-acre Osceola State Forest. Besides the nearby natural beauty of preserves, parks, and springs, the city offers a spectacular reenactment of the Civil War battle of Olustee every February.

Gainesville, lying just off I-75 on State Route 24, is best known as the home of the main campus of the University of Florida. As such it is a center of cultural and educational activities. Connected with the university is the prestigious Shands Teaching Hospital. An area primarily agricultural surrounds the city.

Of interest nearby is the historical site of Cross Creek, the home of Marjorie Kinnan Rawlings, who wrote *The Yearling*. Visitors can see what an early "cracker" house was like, a style that coped well with temperature controls in the time preceding the air conditioner. Many travelers to Gainesville go to see the Devil's Millhopper. That's a giant among sinkholes, measuring 500 feet across and 118 feet in depth. Instead of turning into a lake, as most sinkholes eventually do, Millhopper is filled with a lush growth of plant life.

Average Fahrenheit temperatures and rainfall for representative cities of the region are:

City	January	July	Annual Rainfall
Jacksonville	55.9	82.6	53.46
Gainesville	58.9	81.1	52.45
St. Augustine	57.8	81.0	52.38

The principal newspapers with a net circulation (1987) of 50,000 or more are the *Jacksonville Florida Times Union/Journal* and the *Gainesville Sun*.

County	Population (1980 census)	Area (sq. mi.)	Density (pop./sq. mi.)
1. Alachua	151,348	961(69)*	169.7
2. Baker	15,289	588	26.1
3. Bradford	20,023	305	68.3
4. Clay	67,052	644	112.1
5. Columbia	35,399	789	44.9
6. Duval	570,981	840(63)	734.9
7. Flagler	10,913	504	22.6
8. Nassau	32,894	671	50.6
9. Putnam	50,549	879(76)	62.0
10. St. Johns	51,303	660(51)	84.2
11. Union	10,166	245	42.4

*indicates square miles of water included when the amount exceeds 50 sq. mi.
(Source: *Florida Almanac*)

3. West Coast (the Sun Coast)

The counties bordering on the Gulf of Mexico to the west enjoy warm weather and spectacular sunsets. They abound in the pastel buildings and palm-lined drives of many resorts. They have natural wonders, and wide beaches with shallow slopes and plenty of shells to thrill collectors, and they also have crowds and clogged roads and commercial blight.

I-75, a section of which was recently completed, is the major highway. In the northern portion is Route 19, and in the southern portion Route 41, both of which roughly parallel the interstate. I-4 begins its way to the East Coast in Tampa, and Route 60 crosses the state to the Atlantic Ocean at Vero Beach. Where I-75 conditionally ends near Naples, it joins Alligator Alley crossing the Everglades to Miami. As soon as improvements on the latter are completed, it will become a part of the I-75 system.

Southward from the Crystal River, which is fed by thirty springs, there are many rivers, notably the Caloosahatchee, the Peace, and the Myakka. Of the many natural springs three are outstanding: Homosassa, Weeki Wachee, and Tarpon Springs. Barrier Islands allow boats to use the Intracoastal Waterway from Clearwater to Fort Myers, and shell-built white beaches run in a nearly unbroken line down the entire coast.

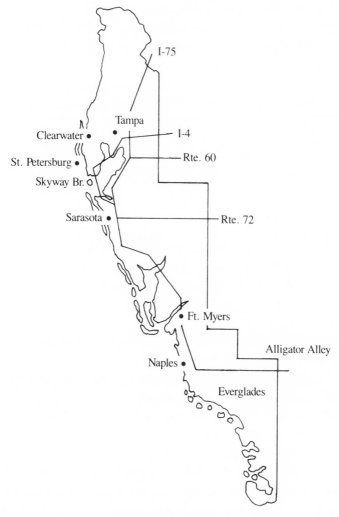

West, the Sun Coast

Tampa is the site of a large port and the location of a variety of businesses. Many of these are desirable nonpolluting industries and corporate offices. It has a beautiful modern airport, cruise ship accommodations, and a military facility, MacDill Air Force Base, to provide extra jobs. Across Tampa Bay the cities of St. Petersburg and Clearwater, Largo and Dunedin, join Tampa to make up a large metropolitan area.

The completion of I-75 opened to rapid growth a 36-mile corridor through formerly rural Hillsborough County. To the north, Pasco County, still mainly quiet residential, is beginning to follow a growth pattern, while Hernando's population has already taken off, growing a spectacular 79% between 1980 and the end of 1987.

In Citrus County, Crystal River is the site of a nuclear power plant, but two of the other springs have been developed for tourists, Weeki Wachee and Homosassa. They provide an opportunity for the public to see the spectacular nature of these wonders, although they're somewhat sanitized and glamorized. Tarpon Springs is unique in that it has a large Greek population and is well known for its sponge diving exhibitions.

In the Tampa Bay area, besides the beaches there are museums and performing arts theaters; the University of South Florida campuses in Tampa and St. Petersburg; Ybor City, an enclave of Spanish culture; Busch Gardens; the replica of H.M.S. Bounty; the Sunken Gardens cultivated in a seventy-foot-deep sinkhole; and the 19-mile engineering feat known as the Sunshine Skyway Bridge that crosses Tampa Bay.

Bradenton is on the mainland at the other end of the bridge. Using a spur of Route 64 you can drive out to Anna Maria Island to enjoy the beauties of its beach. Cultural activities are the highlights of the city of Sarasota, home of Asolo State Theater; the Art Museum, Home and Circus Museum of John Ringling; three formal gardens; and a museum of classic cars. Myakka State Park, fourteen miles to the east, offers 30,000 acres of wildlife refuge with guided tours and transportation within the park.

Venice, winter home of the Greatest Show on Earth, and Englewood, resort towns on the coast, are bypassed by I-75 as it swings eastward around Charlotte Bay. Port Charlotte and Punta Gorda on the northern end of the bay are boating centers for the protected waters, and on the southern side is the city of

Replica of Michelangelo's statue of David in the
Ringling Museum in Sarasota.

Fort Myers. Charlotte Bay is protected from the Gulf of Mexico
by a string of barrier islands. It's fed by the Myakka River that
flows through the state park of the same name and the Peace
River, which comes from the watershed in the Central Region.

Fort Myers, a city of light colors and palm-lined streets, is
situated on yet another major river, the Caloosahatchee, that

arrives from the east near Lake Okeechobee. It offers a jungle cruise up the river to the edge of the wilderness and cross-Florida trips that begin on the Caloosahatchee and end at Fort Pierce on the East Coast. It's the site of the interesting attractions of Thomas Edison's winter home, gardens, and laboratory, and it's also the mainland access point to the causeway leading to two islands known for their strict conservation. The islands, Sanibel and Captiva, are home to many birds and reptiles. It's the only place you'll see a sign warning motorists: "Caution, sea otter crossing." On Sanibel is an excellent site for the observation of nature, the J.N. "Ding" Darling Wildlife Refuge.

From Fort Myers you can take Route 82 to Immokalee, gateway to the Big Cypress Swamp, and then take Route 29 right through the middle of this fascinating wilderness.

Down the coast farther is Naples, a truly subtropical spot. It's a small city at the edge of Big Cypress, featuring elegant mansions reminiscent of the Riviera. Sixteen miles to the south is Marco Island, an isolated and natural environment in the process of growing to be a small city. The Ten Thousand Islands begin here. They aren't made of sand, as you might expect, but they grew from mangrove roots that trapped shells and driftwood and seaweed until the accretion was big enough to make an island. The process of building these islands continues. Some say the true name should now be Twenty Thousand Islands. The town of Everglades City, near the intersection of Route 29 and the Tamiami Trail, is the site of a visitors' center for the Everglades National Park.

Average Fahrenheit temperatures and rainfall for representative cities of this region are:

City	January	July	Annual Rainfall
St. Petersburg	63.3	82.7	55.41
Fort Myers	61.7	82.2	53.44

The principal newspapers with a net circulation (1987) of 50,000 or more are these: *St. Petersburg Times; Tampa Tribune; Fort Myers News Press; Sarasota Herald Tribune.*

County	Population (1980 census)	Area (sq. mi.)	Density (pop./sq. mi.)
1. Charlotte	59,115	832(127)*	83.9
2. Citrus	54,703	661(91)	95.9
3. Collier	85,791	2,119	42.2
4. DeSoto	19,039	721	26.5
5. Hardee	19,379	630	30.8
6. Hernando	44,469	508	91.2
7. Hillsborough	646,960	1,062	622.1
8. Lee	205,266	1,005(786)	261.2
9. Manatee	148,442	772(84)	215.8
10. Monroe	63,098	994(424)	63.5
11. Pasco	194,123	772	258.5
12. Pinellas	728,409	309	2,759.1
13. Sarasota	202,251	563	382.3

*indicates square miles of water included when the amount exceeds 50 sq. mi.
(Source: *Florida Almanac*)

4. Central (the Heartland)

The Central Region begins at Ocala National Forest and runs to the shores of Lake Okeechobee. It is the only area not touching in some part on the sea, but it doesn't lack for waterways since 1,400 of the state's 30,000 lakes are found here. It's still a major citrus growing area in spite of the decline of acreage under cultivation since the killing frosts of December 1983 and January 1985, and where the groves run out the sugar cane begins. The region is probably best known, however, for its tourist attractions.

An exit of I-75 in Sumter County joins the beginning of the 265-mile Florida Turnpike, which runs south to the tip of the state at Florida City, the gateway to the Everglades. At Ocala U.S. 27 begins a parallel route running along a more westerly line. The Beeline Expressway, heading for the Spacecoast, starts at an exit from the Turnpike. I-4 is a major artery for Orlando and nearby attractions as it makes its way from Tampa to Daytona Beach. State Route 50, which joins the east and west coasts, serves much of the growth in the region.

Apopka, the second largest lake in Florida, has suffered the runoff from muck farms and the effluent from residences and is

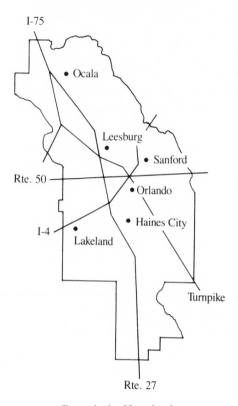

Central, the Heartland

presently undergoing efforts at cleanup. A number of lakes in the area are joined by natural or artificial channels to make up chains, which are most attractive to boaters. Among these are the Harris chain at Leesburg, Butler at Windermere, and those at Clermont, Kissimmee, and Winter Park.

Ocala is one of the three largest cities in the region. It's located near the National Forest and three principal springs: Alexander, Juniper, and Silver Springs. The hiking trail that is projected to run 1,300 miles passes through the forest. It marks the uppermost limit of the citrus belt, and where there are no groves or new developments, a traveler will see the white fences and the beautiful thoroughbreds of the horse farms.

Orlando is another large city. Actually, the city limits are surrounded by many incorporated towns that make up Orlando's metropolitan area. Most persons will not find it a surprise to learn that the city is the hub of the chief tourist attractions. However, the city has attractions of its own, with Leu and Mead Gardens, and Loch Haven Park with its Science Center, museums, and theaters.

When Walt Disney bought 280,000 acres of unexplored swampland to build his Magic Kingdom, the Central Region underwent a profound change. High-rise bank buildings proliferated to pierce Orlando's skies; population mushroomed; new roads became clogged before they were finished; municipal services and schools were strained; housing starts and hotel rooms sent the graphs off the charts. The surrounding counties are acquiring rights of way to build a beltway, which will alleviate some of the traffic, but it's feared this will be only temporary until the land opened up to development by the new road chokes it with additional traffic. Already the Orlando portion of I-4 carries 5% of the traffic of the city, whereas nationwide interstates carry only 1%.

The Magic Kingdom, EPCOT, Lake Buena Vista World Village, Wet and Wild, Mystery Fun House, and Sea World are close enough to be identified with Orlando, but there are other cities with major attractions:

Ocala—Silver Springs
Clermont—Citrus Tower
Winter Haven—Cypress Gardens
Haines City—Boardwalk and Baseball
Kissimmee—Tupperware Headquarters tours and
     theater, Gatorland Zoo, and SST Aviation
     Museum
Lake Wales—Bok Singing Tower
Lake Placid—Happiness Tower

Also being developed on Disney's land is a moviemaking center which will offer tours to visitors beginning in the spring

A citrus grove near Lake Wales.

of 1989. At the same time Disney began this project in conjunction with MGM, Movie Corporation of America/Universal Studios was working on a similar park near Interstate 4 and the Florida turnpike in southwest Orlando. A new water sports attraction called Typhoon Lagoon opened on the Magic Kingdom acreage in 1988. Visitors will probably be pleased to know that a third of the whole Disney tract is to be kept a wildlife refuge; otherwise, a vacation there could be more exhausting than restful.

Small towns have a variety of offerings. Apopka, for example, is known as the foliage capital for its production of house and landscaping plants, a distinction also claimed by Lake Placid. Sanford, site of the Central Florida Zoo, is the southern terminus of the auto-train that runs to the Washington, D.C. beltway, and is the nearest city to facilities for houseboat rental on the St. Johns. Longwood is proud of its 3,500-year-old oak, the Senator, which is 125 feet high and has a trunk 47 feet in circumference. (Can you believe a tree is still alive that was a seedling in 1500 B. C.?)

Winter Park not only is a prestigious address, but it also has the Morse Gallery of Art and Rollins College. State Route 561 passes through Clermont to Lake Louisa State Park. Leesburg offers a large state recreation facility in Lake Griffin, and on its chain of lakes every February a fishing tournament with big-money prizes attracts many anglers; Mt. Dora is an old village turned trendy that annually presents a big art festival. Lake Wales is host city to the Black Hills Passion Play, presented every year during Lent since 1951; Sebring is home to auto races; Lakeland, the third of the large cities of this region, has Florida Southern College and fine medical facilities; and Kissimmee prides itself on its rodeo, an annual boat-a-cade from Lake Tohopekaliga, and its raising of quarter horses.

Average Fahrenheit temperatures and rainfall for representative cities of the region are:

City	January	July	Annual Rainfall
Orlando	60.4	81.5	51.37
Lakeland	61.7	81.6	51.37

The principal newspapers with a net circulation (1987) of 50,000 or more are the *Orlando Sentinel* and the *Lakeland Ledger.*

County	Population (1980 census)	Area (sq. mi.)	Density (pop./sq. mi.)
1. Highlands	47,526	1,119(78)*	45.7
2. Lake	104,870	1,163(167)	105.3
3. Marion	122,488	1,652	75.8
4. Orange	471,660	1,003(87)	514.3
5. Osceola	49,287	1,467(142)	37.2
6. Polk	321,652	2,048(187)	172.8
7. Seminole	179,752	352	559.9
8. Sumter	24,272	574	43.3

*indicates square miles of water included when the amount exceeds 50 sq. mi.
   (Source: *Florida Almanac*)

5. East Central (the Spacecoast)

Barrier islands extend the entire length of the East Central Coast, taking the brunt of the Atlantic's pounding, while the

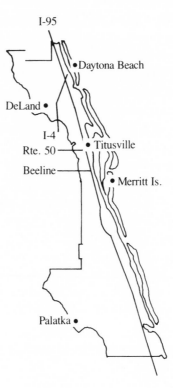

East Central, the Spacecoast

nearby Gulf Stream provides a tempering warmth. The region extends from Daytona Beach south to Stuart, and inland to the Central Region.

The region is served primarily by I-95 and U.S. Route 1 running north and south; by I-4 that terminates at Daytona Beach after arriving from Tampa; by State Route 50 that joins the east and west coasts of the state; and by State Route 528, also known as the Beeline Expressway, that runs from the Florida Turnpike near Orlando to connect with roads to the space center on Cape Canaveral.

It is probably best known for the wide beaches extending from Daytona Beach to New Smyrna, but vying for "best known" is the Kennedy Space Center. Also close to the top of the list is racing, and next must come the famed citrus crop of Indian River.

On the beaches for years the bathers have had to dodge the traffic of the autos allowed to drive and to park there. Because the problem has become more serious with growth, municipalities and counties have formulated new rules to govern access to the beaches. There are daily charges (with concessions to local residents) and restricted hours for cars, effective in Nassau, Volusia, and St. Johns Counties. Some restrictions are being challenged in the courts. Making a solution to the traffic problem more difficult are several concerns: lack of cooperation among the cities in providing uniformity of rules, scarcity of parking facilities off the beach, and the reluctance of localities to interfere with a lucrative activity. There are some beaches that are part of national or state parks, and while the public pays a nominal charge to use these, cars are not permitted. Playalinda, part of Canaveral National Seashore, is one of these.

The "world's most famous" beach on the
Atlantic Ocean at Daytona Beach.

Many tourists visit John F. Kennedy Space Center where comprehensive guided tours are available year-round. But what most visitors may not know is that the Center occupies only one-seventh of the area controlled by the National Aeronautics and Space Agency; the rest is a wildlife refuge, as much like primitive Florida as you can find anywhere. At nearby Cocoa Beach, Patrick Air Force Base maintains a missle display open to the public.

One of auto racing's most famous courses is the Daytona International Speedway. Those fans who arrive when there is no race in progress or whose interests move them can visit the Museum of Speed in Ormond Beach, which has been designated a National Historical Site. Motorcycle clubs convene at Daytona Beach in the spring, and an invasion of half a million college students occurs annually during "spring break."

As a possible resident, you may consider these as minuses, but you can always weigh them against the great pluses of swimming, sunbathing, and boating and fishing in the Intracoastal Waterway.

Some of the finest citrus crops in the state come from Indian River County, of which the principal city is Vero Beach. The fruit crop grown here is often warmed by the winds off the ocean when heavy frost kills crops inland. You might note that the Indian River itself is really a lagoon and part of the intracoastal system.

The principal cities begin with the Ormond, Daytona, and New Smyrna Beaches. Besides the sun and surf, there are commercial amusements and some historical sites to visit. Among the latter are 900-acre Tomoka State Park, Sugar Mills Gardens, and Canaveral National Seashore.

To the west of these cities, off I-4 on the St. Johns River, are found DeLand, Deltona, and DeBary, cities undergoing incredible development, with prices of new homes very competitive. Shopping centers to accommodate the growing population have nearly outstripped the residential growth. DeLand in its quieter days was best known as the site of Stetson University. Close to these cities are two famous springs, DeLeon and Blue Springs. These and adjoining Hontoon Island are popular state parks and recreation areas. One of the special attractions of Blue Springs is the presence of manatees, who winter there to escape the cold waters of the Atlantic. Unfortunately, there they often meet an unnatural enemy: boat propellers. Strict enforcement of protected areas and slow boat speeds don't always work, for the great beasts are very slow-moving and swim under the surface of the water as inconspicuous shadows. The danger is increased when they have to surface to breathe.

Near Titusville, land being checked for archaeological finds before being developed revealed well preserved soft tissues in the buried bodies of early inhabitants. Scientists were surprised at the level of skills represented by artifacts in the graves, and they're particularly interested in examining the DNA and the brain tissue. Titusville is also the gateway to the space center and the Merritt Island National Wildlife Refuge.

Farther south, the city of Melbourne is especially famous for its turtle watches. During July and August these great, gentle sea animals, sometimes weighing up to 700 pounds, come ashore to dig deep holes in the sand above the tide line, where they deposit hundreds of eggs.

In the Fort Pierce area is the St. Lucie Museum State Recreation Area, featuring treasures from sunken ships. There is also an interesting historical museum of Indian artifacts. In the city of Stuart, at the southern end of the region, is the outlet of the St. Lucie Canal. This connects the Intracoastal Waterway with Lake Okeechobee, the largest fresh water lake in Florida. A boat that crosses the lake can then connect by means of locks with the Caloosahatchee River, which flows westward to the Gulf of Mexico at Fort Myers. There are commercial cruise ships that make this trip from Fort Myers to Fort Pierce regularly except in the rare dry seasons when Lake Okeechobee falls below a navigable level.

Average Fahrenheit temperatures and rainfall in representative cities of the region are:

City	January	July	Annual Rainfall
Daytona Beach	59.2	80.1	49.9
Titusville	61.7	81.7	55.96

The principal newspapers with a circulation (1987) of 50,000 or more are *Cocoa Today,* and the *Daytona Beach News Journal.*

County	Population (1980 census)	Area (sq. mi.)	Density (pop./sq. mi.)
1. Brevard	272,959	1,310(279)*	264.8
2. Indian River	59,896	549	116.4
3. Martin	64,014	582	114.5
4. Okeechobee	20,264	780	26.1
5. St. Lucie	87,182	626	148.3
6. Volusia	258,762	1,207(92)	232.0

*indicates square miles of water included when the amount exceeds 50 sq. mi.
(Source: *Florida Almanac*)

6. Southeast (the Gold Coast)

The climate of the Southeast Region is considered the finest in Florida. The days of sunshine and the nearness of the Gulf Stream take the credit. The offshore islands glisten with resort hotels and condominiums that earn it its nickname. There is solid evidence that it isn't only glitter, for in 1987 Dade, Palm Beach, and Broward counties accounted for one-third of the personal income, forty percent of the bank deposits, and one-third of the population of the entire state, according to compilations by the University of Florida Bureau of Economic and Business Research. You won't be surprised to note that the cost of living is highest in the Keys and Dade County.

From Palm Beach to Coral Gables is a megalopolis of sun and sea worshipers. Florida's second largest city, Miami, is its hub. The city has a large Hispanic population, among which, according to an estimate in early 1988, were 700,000 Cubans and 70,000 expatriate Nicaraguans. While they retain the foods and other customs of their homeland, many have been otherwise assimilated into "Anglo" culture, speak English, and live peaceably under the benefits of the laws of the country. The last couple of mayors of the city have been Hispanics.

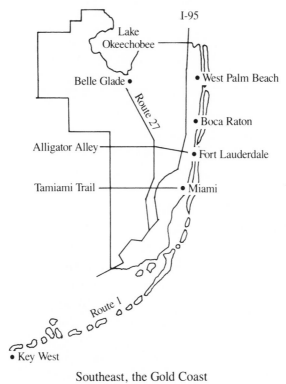

Southeast, the Gold Coast

Miami, however, is also the center through which much of the illegal drug traffic passes, often cleverly disguised as innocuous goods to deceive the customs officials. The fate of the ex-prisoners from Castro's jails that came on the Mariel boatlift is still unsettled. Further social problems arise when poverty-stricken refugees from such countries as Haiti also head for Miami as the nearest gateway to the United States. There has, however, been a marked improvement in the crime picture since the boatlift in 1981. That year there were 576 killings in Dade County while in 1987 there were 376.

There is no doubt that insecurity undermines some of the good life on the Southeast Coast. Nevertheless, there are many desirable areas with a low incidence of crimes. And after all, there is no guarantee of personal safety anywhere in the world. You will not be alone in choosing this section of the state, for housing starts are high, tourism is up, and new high-tech businesses are locating in the cities.

Off the coast is the valuable agricultural land of the muck farms where many of the winter vegetables and fruits for the East Coast are grown.

The main highways in the region are I-95 and A1A, which terminate in Miami; U.S. 27, which began in Ocala and continues through the Everglades to the visitors' center in Flamingo; Route 1, this section of which is a limited access road; Alligator Alley; and the Tamiami Trail, Route 41, named for its connection of Tampa and Miami. One last highway is the unique 160-mile stretch of causeways, bridges, and roads that make up the oversea route to the Keys.

The Intracoastal Waterway runs the length of the coast and all the way to Key West. In addition, two canals run to Lake Okeechobee, one from Miami and the other from Boca Raton.

Inland in the vicinity of Lake Okeechobee are the cane fields and the ghost towns of Old Florida Cracker Country. Okeechobee serves many purposes besides the unhappy role of being the repository of runoff from surrounding homes and farms; it has great bass fishing, many marinas for private and rental boats, and commercial traffic. It has been dredged to carry barges and smaller cargo ships.

Inland, Broward and Dade Counties are covered with the wetlands of the Everglades. Although they aren't part of the national park and are in private hands, they are protected by state laws. Loxahatchee National Wildlife Preserve lies on an extensive plot in Palm Beach County. Western Broward County has tracts designated as reservations for two Indian tribes, the Seminoles and the Miccosukees. All the urban areas lie on a narrow sand belt with a rock base along the coast. Geologists say the base is a continuation of the Appalachian Mountains.

From Jupiter to Key West are found many preserves, Indian mounds, parks, and wildlife refuges.

In Jupiter is the Burt Reynolds' Theater and a 105-foot-high lighthouse that overlooks the Gulf Stream five miles away. The three Palm Beaches are known for the wealthy homes of celebrities and for the Flagler Museum, the Four Arts Gallery, a science museum, a zoo, Lion Country Safari, and the headquarters of the Professional Golf Association.

Delray Beach offers outdoor pleasures and the unique Japanese Morikami Gardens and Museum. Tours are arranged for visits to the interior wetlands at Loxahatchee. Boca Raton is home to Florida Atlantic University. All the places with name recognition, like Deerfield and Pompano Beach, have their individual features, but all share the sun and the sea and the warmth of the Atlantic Coast.

Even among so many resort cities, one stands out: Fort Lauderdale, the "Venice" of the Gold Coast. It has a lovely beach and 250 miles of lagoons and canals that serve the residents as roads. For visitors there are a railroad museum, train tours, a jungle cruise, a state park, and all the city's waterways to explore.

Davie has a weekly rodeo; Hollywood has Six Flags Atlantis water park; Coral Gables, home of the University of Miami, has the Seaquarium, the mysterious Coral Castle that was built by a single reclusive man, and the estate of Vizcaya, a palace built by John Deering, tours of which are open to the public.

And then Miami, with all the amenities of a great city, offers Florida International and Miami Universities, cultural affairs, national sports events, parks and museums, Metrozoo, a great seaport which handles 2.5 million cruise passengers annually, a busy international airport catering to European vacationers, sight-seeing cruises, gardens, beaches with first-class hotels, and the attractions of bilingual culture. The diversity of the city from the impoverished sections to the elegance of high-rise condominiums can be expected in a place the size of Greater Miami, 2,000 square miles.

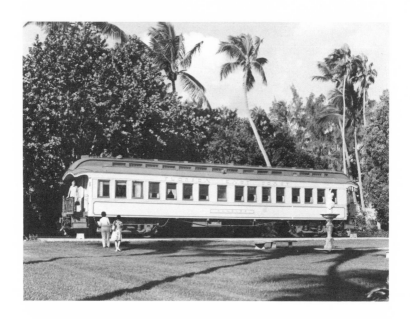

Flagler Museum in Miami, dedicated to the entrepreneur who helped
open up South Florida to settlement.

In contrast there is the quiet backwater town of Florida City.
It lies in the agricultural belt at the edge of the National Park on
the only highway entering it. Leading off from the same town is
Route 1, the highway to the Keys.

The first key on the route is Key Largo, base for underwater
exploring at Biscayne and John Pennekamp Coral Reef State
Parks. Along the way the keys are lightly populated and individualistic. Big Pine Key is the one visitors remember most; it's
home to the Key deer and to the cactus and pine trees that are
not found on other keys. It is unique in that it has the same base
rock as the coast. Marathon has a museum and an attraction
called "Aquadome." Last, of course, you will come to Key
West, its people and its picturesque houses crowded onto its
three by five miles. There you will find the mementoes of Hemingway, the Old Town, the conch (pronounced konk) trains, the
unusual native foods, and the famous sunsets.

You can go even farther west and visit the Dry Tortugas, but you couldn't live there. They are tiny islands beginning eighteen miles west of Key West, named for the turtles that frequented them. One of them is the site of Fort Jefferson, whose most famous prisoner was Dr. Samuel A. Mudd. His "crime" was setting the broken leg of the fugitive John Wilkes Booth, the man who assassinated Lincoln.

Average Fahrenheit temperatures and rainfall for representative cities in the region are:

City	January	July	Annual Rainfall
Miami Beach	69.1	82.3	46.26
Key West	70.4	84,0	39.84
Homestead	65.6	80.2	54.69

The principal newspapers with a net circulation (1987) of 50,000 or more are the *Miami Herald, West Palm Beach Post/ Times,* and the *Fort Lauderdale Sun Sentinel.*

County	Population (1980 census)	Area (sq. mi.)	Density (pop./sq. mi.)
1. Broward	1,014,043	1,220	832.5
2. Dade	1,625,977	2,109(55)*	791.6
3. Glades	5,992	898(152)	8.0
4. Hendry	18,599	1,189	15.7
5. Palm Beach	573,125	2,578(600)	283.7

(The Keys are part of Monroe County.)

*indicates square miles of water included when the amount exceeds 50 sq. mi.

(Source: *Florida Almanac*)

Before you settle for good on your retirement location, be sure to check the area for yourself. Ask the other retirees who live there. You'll find them a friendly, talkative lot. And don't expect perfection. Anywhere you live will be a compromise; if it's in a city there will be convenience, but also crowding; if it's close to one place, it will be farther from another.

Read on, too, please. This book will help you choose the best kind of home for you, will explain some of the laws, and will familiarize you with the vagaries of the weather. It will offer up-to-date statistics on such topics as the cost of living and your life expectancy. It will recount the history and describe the environment and the indigenous wildlife. Hopefully it will answer many questions.

There is a caveat, however. Although the material in the book came from reliable sources and was valid when it was written, things have a habit of changing. Anything true today may become untrue tomorrow. New cures are found; new laws are passed; new theories are proven; new perceptions change the outlooks of both reader and writer. But you know that; otherwise, you wouldn't have survived to retirement age!

Good hunting.

2. *Getting Acquainted*

A look at the neighborhood

Before you make your home in Florida, you'll want to learn some facts about the state. It's as different from any other state among the fifty as are Alaska and Hawaii. It's as far south as you can get in the continental United States, yet the population is predominantly from the North. It has the longest coastline and the lowest elevation on the continent. In the Everglades it has an ecosystem unique in the world, and it has water problems that threaten it. It has the most delicately balanced environment and one of the most mistreated. It has natural beauty and destructive hurricanes.

A look at the map will show you some surprising things. For example, Florida's *northern border* extends 600 miles farther south than the southernmost point in California, which is why Florida's climate is sometimes described as semitropical and Southern California's as subtropical. The westernmost city, Pensacola, is on the same meridian as Chicago. If you're looking at a globe or a world map, you'll find that Miami is in the same latitude as Cairo, Egypt; Riyadh, Saudi Arabia; Karachi, Pakistan; Taipei, Taiwan; and Benares, India.

In size Florida is 22nd among the states, but second among those east of the Mississippi. Its total area is 58,560 square miles, which includes 4,470 square miles of water. A gull flying down the length of the Atlantic coast would cover 580 miles, but the actual miles of shoreline including offshore islands, sounds, bays, and the tidal portion of rivers, is 3,331 miles. That means there are 5.7 miles of beach for each air mile of coastline. Similarly, the Gulf Coast is 770 miles in length, but has 5,095 miles of tidal shoreline. Not only is that a lot of sand and surf, but no matter where you choose to live in Florida you can never be farther than seventy miles from a coast and more likely will be closer than forty.

There are two time zones in the state and three temperature belts. The northern section gets a dusting of snow now and then; the central portion is subject to occasional frost; and the southern tip is subtropical. Key West is the only city in the continental United States that has never recorded freezing temperatures. Within the borders of the 67 counties are 30,000 named lakes.

Geologically speaking, Florida is the youngest portion of North America. It also has the lowest profile, for the highest elevation in the state is less than 350 feet. At one time 90% of the land was covered by forest.

Florida was acquired from Spain by treaty in 1821 and was classified as a territory. On March 3, 1845, it became the 27th state to enter the Union. It has expressed its individuality (and sometimes its absurdity) by adopting these symbols through actions of the state legislature:

> State motto: "In God We Trust"
> Song: "Old Folks at Home" ("Suwannee River")
> Day: April 2 (first landing on the coast)
> Nickname: Sunshine State
> Flower: orange blossom
> Tree: sabal palm
> Bird: mockingbird
> Animal: Florida panther

Seashell: horse conch
Saltwater fish: Atlantic sailfish
Freshwater fish: largemouth bass
Marine mammal: manatee
Saltwater mammal: porpoise
Reptile: alligator
Gem: moonstone
Beverage: orange juice
Dessert: Key lime pie
Stone: agatized coral
Play: Cross and Sword (at St. Augustine)
Theater: Asolo (in Sarasota)

The state flag has crossed diagonal bands of bright red on a white ground. In the center is the state seal, which pictures an Indian standing by a body of water over which the sun is shining. Indigenous plants and a sailing ship complete the picture.

If you're interested in finding new friends, the concentration of people around your age is highest in Florida. By 1990 one-fifth of the population will be 65 or older, according to a study by Florida International University. The researchers also offer the estimate that those *85 and over* will double in two years to 372,000. Of course, many new retirees aren't yet 65, but the 55-65 age group has an even higher share of the population.

Another way to measure the number of retirees is to look at the figures on those receiving Social Security (although a small number of the total are dependents of deceased insureds). In 1985 the average per 1,000 for the nation was 51; in Florida it was 203. On the last day of 1986 there were 2,380,980 Florida recipients, whose average benefit was $487.49 a month.

The American Association of Retired Persons, a very popular organization that was growing by 14,000 new members every working day in 1988, reports over 2 million of its members live in Florida. If you're interested in joining, the administrative offices of the national headquarters are at 1909 K St. NW, Washington, DC 20049. The membership processing center is at

3200 E. Carson St., Lakewood CA, 90712. The organization is a powerful voice in the halls of Congress, and in addition offers many services, such as health insurance, group travel, investments, and pharmaceuticals.

It's interesting to learn a little about the people who lived here before you came. The story begins in pre-Columbian times.

A brief history

At least 14,000 years ago Indians moved into Florida. By the time Europeans discovered the land there were an estimated 50,000 to 75,000 of them living in half a dozen major tribes. In the northeast were the Timucuans, and in the Panhandle the Apalachees, both of which chiefly engaged in agriculture and hunting. Two warlike tribes, the Ais and the Jeagis, made their homes farther down the Atlantic Coast. The Calusas, in the area of Charlotte Harbor on the Gulf Coast, were warriors known to practice human sacrifice, and the Tekestas, who lived on the Keys, were primarily fishermen.

They all had many skills in addition to planting and hunting: they could weave cloth, engage in graphic and decorative arts, practice religion, live in an organized society under the rule of a cacique (chief) and a council, domesticate animals, observe burial customs, dance and play music, use herbs and rituals as medicine, and build shelters of wood and reeds.

Although it is believed that an Englishman, John Cabot, probably visited the coast in 1498, the first attempt to settle Florida was by the Spaniards. Tristan de Luna established a settlement in the Pensacola Bay area in 1559, but it lasted only two years. St. Augustine, founded in 1565 by Pedro Menendez de Aviles, is the oldest city in North America.

Juan Ponce de Leon was a nobleman at the court of Spain who sailed to the New World with Columbus on his second voyage in 1493 and became very interested in exploration. Because the king regarded him highly for his having fought bravely in the Moorish Wars, he was made governor of some of the Caribbean Islands. In Bimini he heard that there was great wealth to the north, as well as a fountain of healing waters, and he set out to find them.

On Easter Sunday, March 27, 1513, he sighted the Atlantic Coast near the present city of St. Augustine. He landed on April 2nd and claimed it for the King of Spain, naming it La Florida after the Spanish words for the flowering of Easter. Following the coast, he explored farther, fought a battle with the Ais, and reported the first sighting of the Gulf Stream. He sailed around the Keys, visited and named the Dry Tortugas, and continued as far north as Sanibel, near the present city of Fort Myers. After he returned home he was knighted by the king and sent back as governor of La Florida. In 1521 he was wounded in a battle with the Calusas and died soon afterward.

Many explorers followed him. Their names are familiar: Pizzaro, Cortes, De Soto, Coronado, Narvaez, Cabeza de Vaca. These men were searching for gold and personal gain, and they were much more successful in achieving their goals in Mexico and Central and South America than they were in Florida.

Spanish treasure recovered from wrecks in the Gulf of Mexico.

De Soto's search took him through ten of the present states, as far north as Tennessee and as far west as Texas. His route was so well documented by journals that it has been traced through the various states with great accuracy. For example, it is recorded that in 1539 ten ships carrying 622 Spaniards under his command landed in Tampa Bay and set out to explore, eventually traveling as far west as Texas. By the time the explorers returned, floating down the Mississippi River, four years had passed and their numbers had dwindled to 311.

Cabeza de Vaca likewise left eye-witness accounts for historians. His story is full of hardships and hairbreadth escapes as he went as far westward as California in his search for the fabled Seven Golden Cities of Cibola.

The conquistadores were fanatical in their search for wealth, and sent many cargoes home to Spain from Central America. However, King Philip II was disillusioned with Florida. No gold had been found, and there was little profit in trade goods. Hundreds of ships were lost either to weather or to pirates. In 1561 he ordered the establishment of three military bases as refuges for his ships, and otherwise planned to stop throwing good money after bad in that part of the New World. That is, until the French came the next year and claimed land in the name of King Charles IX.

It was a time of religious upheaval in Europe. The Reformation caused many to break away from the Catholic Church, and the persecution of defectors led to their desire to escape by emigration. The Huguenots of France under Jean Ribaut were the first to flee to the New World to seek freedom to practice their religion. Despite the fact that at least two settlements were made, they were short-lived, for these colonists, too, suffered hunger and shipwreck. When the Spanish resumed their claim by sending colonists to found St. Augustine, the remaining French had died or given up.

Meanwhile, pirates freely raided the "Plate Fleet," Spanish vessels carrying gold and valuable supplies of fur and sugar and wood to Spain. The Indians continued to rebel, hating the harshness of the Spanish and resisting the Christianity the priests tried to impose on them. Next the English began to colonize land that Spain claimed along the Atlantic Coast. The first such settlement was by Sir Walter Raleigh in Roanoke in 1585. When St. Augustine was attacked by a British corsair, Spain was again forced to pay some attention to its neglected colony.

As Spanish influence declined, it was replaced by the rising interest of other European countries. The French concentrated on Mobile and New Orleans; the English moved south to Savannah. Eventually there were clashes between these two rivals, also. In the Seven Years' War, which broke out in 1762, Britain defeated both Spain and France. (In our history books this is called the French and Indian War.) Spain gave up Florida for Havana, and France ceded Canada to Britain. The success of the English came mainly from the strength of the settlements they made—they came to find homes rather than wealth.

After two hundred years of Spanish rule, when the British set up a western capital at Pensacola, there were only 100 huts in

Reenactment of the British occupation of the Castillo de San Marcos at St. Augustine.

the city. The eastern capital at St. Augustine had 900 homes and a population of 3,200. The town of Mobile had 350 souls. But there were two million Englishmen and 400,000 slaves in the New World. They built roads, made overtures to the Indians, gave land to both soldiers and officers, and encouraged the production of cash crops such as naval stores, indigo, sugar, rice, cotton, oranges, grapes, and mulberries.

Their troubles came from the same enterprising spirits of their people that had allowed them to succeed where others had failed. The American Colonies rebelled. Florida wasn't directly involved in the Revolution, but it became a hideout for Loyalists, a source of supplies and a base of operations for the British. Because of this, its borders were subject to raids by the rebels. The British had their share of other problems: Indians and runaway slaves, French commercial competition, pirate raids. In 1783 after the Revolution England gave up and ceded Florida back to Spain, upsetting the colonists who had already settled there.

The Second Spanish period fared little better than the first. They inherited the troubles the English had left, and in addition they felt the pressures of the citizens of the United States, who kept moving in and trying to push Florida's boundary line farther south. They even sent their army in to invade the pirate stronghold at Fernandina in Spanish territory. The differences weren't settled until the Treaty of 1819. Finally ratified two years later, it provided five million dollars of reparation to Spain and the cession of Florida to the United States.

While this was happening, the fate of certain Indians affected the future of Florida. In the War of 1812 the Creek tribes took advantage of the preoccupation of the United States to rebel. Their power was broken by men fighting under Gen. Andrew Jackson, and many fled to Florida. These breakaway Creeks were known as "separated people," and an Anglicized version of the Indian word is Seminole. When they got there, their old lands were occupied by white men, and they went on the warpath. In 1817 Jackson crossed the borders to fight them on the

Suwannee River and in Pensacola. He succeeded in putting down what has become known as the First Seminole War. A treaty gave the Indians money, cattle, and hogs to give up their land and move south of the source of the St. Johns and east of Tampa Bay on four million acres near Charlotte Harbor and the Everglades. It was two years after this that Florida became a United States territory.

Jackson was named the first governor and proved to be a great administrator. He established courts, laws, boards of health, schools, and a system of taxes. His was a military government in keeping with the strong arm tactics that he had used in warfare. The population was meager, just 8,000 including slaves. Two thousand of these lived in St. Augustine, and between that city and Pensacola there was a vast wildnerness inhabited by Indians, runaway slaves, and wild animals.

By 1824 roads joined the two capitals although most travel in the state was still by boat. Eleven counties had been formed. To make it easier to govern, Jackson chose Tallahassee as the site of the capital, more or less halfway between Pensacola and St. Augustine. It had all of fifty houses, one church, two hotels, and half a dozen shops owned by skilled artisans. Farms entirely surrounded the town, but as the Indians moved out, new settlers moved in and the town grew rapidly. In the west the principal towns of any size were Quincy, Monticello, Marianna, Madison, and Apalachicola; in the east, Palatka and Jacksonville.

One of the difficulties settlers encountered was finding a valid title to their land. Because land grants had been made by Spain and Britain and the United States, there were often conflicts in deciding who owned what. The courts were kept busy hearing these claims. It's interesting to know that in 1826 the average going price for an acre of Florida land was $1.25.

Soon settlers began encroaching on some of the lands to which the Indians had been sent, and efforts were made to move them out again, this time to vacant lands in the West, mainly in the present state of Oklahoma, known then as Indian Territory. Suffering from restraints, crop failures, and pressure from the whites, the Seminoles agreed to send their chiefs to inspect the land to the west, and if they accepted it, to move at the rate of one-third of their number a year. Not all the Indians agreed to the treaty: Osceola and Micanopy were the leaders of the defiant. In fact, when Osceola was asked to sign, he stuck his knife in the document instead and eloquently expressed his bitterness at the perfidy of the white men.

Nevertheless, the Secretary of War sent negotiators to move the Indians by force. They repudiated the treaty, and just before the deadline they attacked Fort King in Tampa Bay, the assembly point for their exodus. The Second Seminole War had begun. It lasted from 1837 to 1842, when most of the Indians were relocated on Western lands. No peace treaty was signed. Technically the war has never ended. Nor did Osceola surrender. Instead he was taken prisoner by trickery, having accepted negotiations under a flag of truce. Taken to Fort Moultrie, South Carolina, where his grave is today, he starved himself. In the bloody war 1,500 white soldiers gave their lives, and the government spent $40,000,000.

There had been an estimated 4,000 Indians and 1,000 blacks, who were held as their slaves, in the territory in 1822. The descendants of those who were left after 1842 live mostly on one of four reservations in the state: Immokalee, Hollywood, Brighton, and Big Cypress Swamp. These sites are wetlands that retain their primitive characteristics. Some natives still live in traditional homes built on platforms raised above the water level, with open sides and palm thatched roofs. Such dwellings are called chickees.

The Seminoles continue to hunt and fish and preserve their folkways, raise cattle, sell trinkets, sponsor lucrative bingo games, and try to retain their identity in the modern world. They gave their names to many places in the state. Below are a few:

Hialeah	Pretty prairie
Homosassa	Where wild pepper grows
Loxahatchee	Turtle river
Okahumpka	Bitter water

Palatka	Boat crossing
Yalaha	Oranges
Yeehaw	Wolf

Between 1830 and 1840 the population of Florida grew 57%. Congress encouraged immigration by offering free land south of a line drawn between Palatka and Gainesville. Agriculture boomed. The major crops were citrus, cotton, sugar cane, tobacco, indigo, wood from live oak and cedar trees, hides, pelts, tallow, and beeswax. The citrus crop suffered a setback in February of 1835 when a freeze registered − 7 degrees Fahrenheit in St. Augustine, but eventually new trees were planted and flourished.

During this period the constitutional convention was held to arrange Florida's admission as a state. At the time statehood was achieved, the population was 58,000, including 25,000 slaves. The first governor, William D. Moseley, received a salary of $1,500 a year.

In 1849 the Seminoles went on the warpath for the third time. They were protesting their treatment by some of the soldiers. After the brief rebellion was put down, more of their number migrated West.

Fifteen years after Florida was admitted to the Union, she seceded and fought on the side of the Confederacy. Her ports were blockaded, but the Union fleet couldn't blanket the area totally, and some blockade runners got through. The people had to pay heavy taxes and find substitutes for everyday goods and grieve for their lost sons, but there was only one major battle on their soil. This is known as the Battle of Olustee, a town a few miles east of Lake City. Five thousand Union troops, including 1,600 black soldiers, were repulsed after a bloody battle. The North had 1,861 casualties including killed, wounded, and missing in action, while the South suffered half as many. The fight is reenacted at the site on the anniversary of the battle every February.

Florida contributed 15,000 soldiers to the Confederate Army and 2,200 to the Union. A thousand died on the battlefields and 5,000 were wounded.

Reconstruction was a sad period everywhere in the South. There were feelings of humiliation and divided loyalties, debts to pay, the invasion of carpetbaggers, the shortages of food, the rise of the Ku Klux Klan, the problems of dealing with the freed but uneducated slaves. Among other woes was money owed to railroads and for the settlement of Indian war claims. The state was reduced to selling four million acres of wetlands at 25 cents an acre.

Recovery came, however. Travel was still mostly by stagecoach and boats, but the railroads were moving in. By 1900, 3,500 miles of track had been laid. The era of the wealthy industrialist had arrived, and C. W. Plant, John D. Rockefeller, and Henry M. Flagler were among the wealthiest. They had investments in agriculture, steamship lines, hotels, and railroads. They built expensive homes and engaged in philanthropic endeavors.

The southern part of the state was opened to development in 1896 by Flagler's building of a railroad to Miami, then just a small town. The population was so sparse that mail delivery was accomplished by runners who ran along the beaches carrying their shoes, the so-called barefoot mailmen. Of course, in no time the newly accessible natural beauty and climate of the area caused its population to mushroom. Flagler went a step further in 1905 when he began extending his road over 128 miles of water and islands to Key West. After many bouts with heat and insects, and with the labor of 3,000 men, it was completed in 1912.

The era of land speculation followed the railroads and the miracle of the automobile. Enticing ads appeared in the Northern papers touting the benefits of Florida living, often offering for sale undeveloped swamp lands. The land boom reached its height after World War I and never slowed until the stock market crash of 1929. Some of it still goes on today, for greed knows no season, but there are legal protections for the unwary and more sophistication among prospective buyers.

Homeseekers'

Round-Trip

Excursions

—— TO THE ——

EAST COAST OF FLORIDA

From Ohio and Mississippi River Gateways and also
from Chicago and Other Points In Central
Passenger Association Territory

—— ON THE ——

FIRST AND THIRD TUESDAY EACH MONTH MAY TO NOVEMBER, 1906

Tickets good for 21 days, which gives ample time to examine the best locations
along the Florida East Coast Railway. For further particulars
ask your nearest ticket agent or address

FLORIDA EAST COAST RAILWAY   130 EAST ADAMS STREET
CHICAGO, ILL.

Via ALL RAILROADS

On first and third Tuesdays of each month.

Apply to your ticket agent for further particulars, or to

L. LARSON, Northwestern Agent,

Florida East Coast Railway,

130 Adams Street,   CHICAGO, ILL.

An advertisement of the Florida East Coast Railway in 1906 to encourage
development of south Florida.

Florida State Archives

Now that you have a background of information about the state, you're probably anxious to turn to more practical things. The following chapter, called "Settling In," is the logical next step.

3. *Settling In*

Moving, besides being tiring, is an uncertain time. There are so many things to learn about your new situation in so short a time. Let's try to clear up some concerns of the business of everyday life that new residents have to face: the neighbors, the weather, laws and taxes, medical care, and matters of money.

Population

Among items to note in the later years of its history is Florida's phenomenal growth. Here are the census figures taken from the *1988 Florida Statistical Abstract:*

1830	34,730
1870	187,748
1910	752,619
1930	1,468,211
1950	2,771,305
1970	6,791,418
1980	9,746,324
1987(est.)	12,000,000

Some figures from the *Abstract* and the U.S. Census of 1980 concerning sex, race, and age are also interesting.

Proportion: males 5.6 to females 6.0
white 9.9 to black 1.7

Age	Population
60-64	564,652
65-59	579,012
70-74	480,141
75+	628,420

The following figures comparing Florida with the total population of the United States are taken from the 1980 census:

	Florida	United States
Total population	9,746,324	226,546,000
Median age	34.7	30.0
% 65 or older	17.3	11.3
% Black race	13.8	11.7
% Hispanic	8.8	6.4
Median family income	$17,326	$19,908
Median household size	2.55	3.11

The table of your life expectancy that follows was taken from the *Florida Statistical Abstract*. It tells how many more years of life remain:

	Male		Female	
Age	Florida	U.S.	Florida	U.S.
50	24.5	23.1	30.2	28.0
60	17.5	15.9	21.7	19.7
70	11.7	10.2	14.0	12.4
80	6.9	5.9	7.7	6.8

The elderly population isn't evenly distributed. It's highest incidence is in Sarasota, 30%, followed by other urban areas clustered about the following cities: Bradenton, West Palm Beach, Fort Myers, Daytona Beach, Fort Lauderdale, St. Petersburg, Fort Pierce, and Ocala, 17.1%.

The weather

The best way to describe Florida weather is to say it's fickle. While the state honestly deserves its nickname of "Sunshine," it's also noted for its storms and for the speed with which one changes into the other. Let's see some of the reasons for its unique climate.

Perhaps you noticed that many of the places in the world in the same latitude are deserts—Cairo and Riyadh, for example—while Florida enjoys more than 50 inches of rainfall a year. The difference is accounted for by the seas that surround Florida and the easterly trade winds that flow over them. As the winds pass over the land, there are no mountains to inhibit them and they absorb heat and rise. When they're high enough in the atmosphere, they cool and drop their moisture.

Since the land has less heat to warm the winds in winter, that's the dry season. The rains of summer usually follow a predictable pattern based on the mechanics of convection currents. In the morning the sky is blue and cloudless; in mid-morning little puffs of clouds appear around the horizon, and as the day progresses they grow into whipped cream piles of cumulus clouds. As the temperature rises, the moisture accumulates in the clouds. By early afternoon the sun is winking in and out of the obscuring mass, and the white billows are darkening into thunderheads. In the middle of the afternoon rains pound down for an hour or two. Most of the rain sinks into the sandy soil, and the sun, moving down the western sky, quickly dries up the remaining puddles.

Humidity is a much more persistent phenomenon. It makes its presence felt day and night in the summer and many days in the winter. If you enjoy the comfort of spending time outdoors, you will have to pay with the discomfort of humidity. Air holds more moisture when it's hot. The annual relative humidity averages 75%. That's enough to make a temperature of 80 degrees feel like 85; 90 degrees feel like 105; and 95 degrees feel like 115.

How does the government operate?

Florida has an unusual executive branch on the state level. Its governor gets most of his clout from his title and visibility throughout the state, but in practice he is more like the chairman of the board of a corporation. The "directors" are the six elected cabinet officials: secretary of state, attorney general, comptroller and banking commissioner, treasurer and insurance commissioner, commissioner of education, and commissioner of agriculture. The governor has one vote, as has each of the cabinet members. He can veto actions of the cabinet only when it is sitting as the pardons board. Of course, he has the right to veto bills passed by the legislature.

The legislature is composed of 42 senators and 121 representatives on a one-man-one-vote basis chosen in single-member districts. They meet for a 60-day regular session in April every year, but frequently extend the law-making time with special sessions.

A redistricting plan based on the 1980 census came from the legislature in 1982. Florida had gained four seats in the House of Representatives, giving it a total of 19, and shifts in population had made it necessary to draw new lines for the state legislature and senate. The criteria for the new districts were size of population (81,200 per district), regional compatibility, and county boundaries. The consensus of opinion is that the legislature came close to the best possible redistricting.

Further reapportionment will have to be made in 1992. Based on present estimates of population, Michigan, New York, Ohio, and Pennsylvania will each lose two seats in the House. California is expected to add four, and Texas and Florida should gain three each.

Voting diversity in Florida causes a problem for candidates. Once the state was solidly Democratic, but now nearly every voter has come from another state or even another country. Going to the ballot box are voters with such disparate backgrounds as newly naturalized Hispanics, retirees from the Northeast and the Midwest, and conservative traditionalists from the Old South. Analysts say that swing voters are probably the key.

Florida is among the top ten states in the nation in the percentage of women in the state legislature. It had 20% in 1988, while the national average was 15%. However, it did not support the equal rights amendment that was narrowly defeated a few years ago.

Forty-eight percent of the registered voters cast ballots in the 1984 statewide election, according to the *1988 Statistical Abstract of the U.S.* Interestingly, on the Gold Coast, which has one-third of the population of the state, senior citizens account for half the vote. There is no question of the importance throughout the state of the concerned voting registration and participation of the over-65 age group.

The third branch of the government, the courts, is set up with seven justices of the Supreme Court, each serving a six-year term, meeting in Tallahassee. Below them are the appellate courts, divided into five districts; twenty circuit courts; and 67 county courts. The appellate courts operate with three judges hearing arguments on each case. Depending on the nature of the case in the lower courts, it may be heard by a judge alone or a jury of six or twelve members.

The state has a "sunshine" law that requires meetings of government entities be open to the public. While this assures access to the meetings, pleasing the public and the press, it also provides for full financial disclosure by public officials, who say it discourages good men from seeking office. Not related to that law, except by verbal association is the "sunset" law. The latter provides that laws on the books last only for a limited time, and if the legislature wishes them to continue, they must reenact them.

Voting

The minimum voting age is 18. The only other requirements are that you be a citizen of the United States and a legal resident of Florida.

To become a legal resident you file a declaration of domicile at the office of the circuit court *or* register to vote at the registration office in the courthouse or with traveling registrars, who appear at commercial and civic centers for that purpose. As soon as you take one of these actions, you are considered a legal resident and are eligible to vote; however, registration rolls are sealed thirty days before an election, so you might have to sit the first one out.

For certain benefits you must be a resident for varying lengths of time. For example, to be employed by the state or a county, you must have been a resident for a year. The same applies to eligibility for jury duty or admission to a state mental institution or for reduced tuition fees at a state institution for higher learning. For Old Age Assistance five years of residency are required.

Primaries are held in September, any necessary run-offs in October, general elections in November, most municipal elections in December, and a preferential presidential primary in March of appropriate years. Florida is one of the Southern states participating in "Super Tuesday." Movements are underway to reduce the number of fall elections by consolidating them to two.

Laws and regulations for drivers

One of the first things you will probably do in Florida after you have registered to vote is to consider changing your car license. You need a documentary title, which you can obtain by showing proof of ownership at the county tag office. The cost of the title depends on the weight of your car. In 1988 these were:

2,500 pounds or less	$18.60
2,501 to 3499 pounds	$26.60
3,500 pounds or more	$36.60

An additional charge of $3.00 is made for the plate, which is changed every five years, and if you transfer your title from another state, the cost is either $7.00, $9.00, or $11.00.

Please understand that there have been efforts to increase these fees and to add a steep impact fee for the first registration of new cars entering the state. The taxes so raised would be dedicated to building the new roads necessary because of the influx of new residents.

Tags must be renewed annually on the birthday of the principal driver or head of the household. When you apply at the tax office, bring along proof of insurance coverage. To avoid standing in line you have the option of paying by mail, but you must enclose a photocopy of your insurance card. The present law requires only that you carry personal injury protection, and beginning in 1989 a modest amount of property damage coverage.

To prepare for your driver's test, you should study the "Florida Driver's Handbook" available from the Department of Highway Safety and Motor Vehicles, Division of Motor Vehicles, Neil Kirkman Building, Tallahassee, Fl 32301. The testing centers also have copies for free distribution to prospective drivers.

To apply for your first-time Florida license to operate a car, you must bring two documents proving your age. Among these can be: out-of-state driver's license, birth certificate, passport, military ID card, school records, an insurance policy more than two years old, a marriage certificate, voter registration card, or other acceptable evidence. You must take a 40-question written test, a vision test, an informal hearing check, and a 20-minute road test. The last of these is given at the discretion of the licensing clerk. A computer check will be made to see whether you have any outstanding unpaid fines, a suspended license, or any other impediments.

If you fail any portions of the tests, they may be taken over again for an additional fee, but in some cases not on the same day.

There were almost 10 million drivers with Florida licenses on the last day of 1986. That means long lines at the license offices. You will save time by making an appointment that will get you into a special line that moves quickly. Call ahead, preferably early in the day, for it seems the phones never stop ringing.

Your personal driving license is renewed annually on your birthday, but you may not have to take a test every year. "Safe drivers"—those without traffic violations or accidents in the last three years—may renew by mail for four years. Follow the instructions on your renewal card and send the fee where directed. In 1988 the cost for a year's license to drive a car was $15.00. You can also qualify for a license good for *six* years, but you must appear in person for an eye examination when your first four-year card has expired, and at that time, according to the judgment of the examiner, you could be retested on the driving range.

If you change your address, you must notify the state within ten days. To avoid the annoyance of long lines, mail your new address, old address, and license number to: Division of Driver Licenses, Neil Kirkman Building, Tallahassee, Fl 32301. That will get your address change into the computer, but you will be wise to place one of your new address labels on the back of your license.

A law went into effect in 1987 requiring driving restraints for children up to five years in any part of a car and seat belts for the driver and the passenger beside him. In spite of pressure from motorcyclists, the law requiring them to wear helmets remained in force in 1988. A bill passed in the 1988 legislative session prohibits drinking from open containers while driving.

Florida permits a right turn on red if no sign forbidding it is posted. The driver must bring the car to a full stop and observe other laws of the right of way before making such a turn. Whenever it's raining hard enough to use windshield wipers, the law requires you to turn on full lights.

There are strict penalties for driving after consuming too much alcohol or being under the influence of drugs. For the *first* conviction a driver's license will be revoked for six months to a year; the fine will be between $250 and 500; imprisonment may be up to six months and probation at least a year; 50 hours of community service may be required; and the guilty driver can be required to attend courses in substance abuse. Also levied on the convicted driver are court costs, and if he has caused personal injury or property damage, he faces a criminal or civil court case.

If you buy a new car in Florida and find that it has an excessive number of flaws, it may qualify for repair or replacement under the "lemon law." The first of these, enacted in 1983, didn't prove very effective, and in 1988 it was strengthened to read that after four attempts fail to repair a flaw, the buyer can ask for a hearing by state arbitrators who are empowered to require replacement or refund of purchase price.

Probably you will not be satisfied to carry only the required insurance coverage. The major insurance companies are nationwide, and the policy you will be offered in Florida will no doubt be familiar to you. The rates will vary with the value of the car, the area in which you live, the number of miles you drive, your age, and the kind of coverage you want. Shop around for prices, or write to the Insurance Commissioner, the Capitol, Tallahassee, Fl 32301, for information about competitive rates called the "Insurance Shopper's Guide." You can also call one of the district offices, which are found in principal cities.

If you take a two-day 55-Alive Safe Driving Course offered by the American Association of Retired Persons (AARP), you can qualify for a 5% reduction in certain coverages in your insurance premiums for three years. After that, a refresher course will earn you the same reduction for another three years. These courses are prepared by the Department of Motor Vehicles and are taught by volunteers. There is a nominal charge for course materials. The Association would welcome more teachers for the project.

You face heavy traffic in many areas, for, according to the Florida Highway Patrol's figures, there were 10.2 million licensed drivers as of January 1, 1988. Of these, nearly 450,000 were over the age of 50. The state was eighth in the country for the number of vehicles per thousand of population.

In 1982 the law requiring annual car inspections of all vehicles expired and wasn't renewed. In 1988, however, inspections were reinstated for pollution due to high emission levels in six urban counties: Broward, Duval, Dade, Hillsborough, Pinellas, and Palm Beach. The action may be extended to other counties, for if the air quality doesn't meet federal standards, the state will lose funds for highways, and new factories could be prohibited from operating in those areas.

You'll like some special advantages of driving in Florida. For one thing, there's no severe frost to break up the road surfaces into potholes. For another, the fact that no snowplows are needed allows for the permanent installation of road reflectors to outline lanes. There are no "bridge freezing" warnings either, of course.

On the other hand, be sure to buy yourself a bug screen and a deflector, or you'll spend a great deal of time cleaning your windshield.

Preparing a will

If you become a Florida resident, you can make a new will or take the one you brought with you to a lawyer. For a minimum charge he will advise of its legality and have it re-witnessed to assure its validity.

Since Florida has no inheritance tax of its own, you will probably be smart to move your property and assets to your new home state. After you have declared your residency, your assets are also no longer subject to income tax in the state from which you moved, although your real property there is still liable. Banks which hold accounts for you should be notified of the change so that they won't withhold interest for state taxes.

When you're preparing the stipulations you want the lawyer to include in your will, you should be aware of an important restriction on the disposition of your homestead. If one of the heads of a family dies without leaving children, the surviving spouse gets title to the homestead regardless of any contrary provision in the will of the decedent. If there are minor children, the spouse retains possession for his or her lifetime before it passes to the children. In case the home is in both names as tenants by the entirety, it passes to the surviving spouse exclusively.

In addition to the right to the homestead property, the surviving spouse has other rights. These include application to the probate court for entitlement to a 30% share of the fair market value of the net estate after a few exclusions. Allowances may also be granted for current expenses, for tangible property such as furniture and automobiles, and for certain personal effects of the deceased.

Because of these laws there are complications when senior citizens contract marriages after the death of their previous spouses. Such marriages are not uncommon. To circumvent the laws and to provide for the children of their former marriages, seniors contemplating marriage often sign premarital agreements. If these are drawn up in a legal manner—and they should be done with the advice of a lawyer—they are recognized as valid by the state.

Every state has laws to outline the precedence of heirs in case there is no will to direct distribution of the decedent's estate. The following are in effect in Florida:

(1) equal shares among the widow or widower and children; or

(2) if no children, entire estate to surviving spouse; or

(3) if no spouse survives, entire estate divided equally among the children; or

(4) if neither spouse nor children nor heirs of the children survive, then the entire estate goes to the parents of the decedent; or

(5) if none of these survive, then the estate passes to brothers and sisters or their descendants; or

(6) if no relatives survive, the state of Florida receives the estate by escheat.

While you're planning the disbursement of your worldly goods, you might like to make a "living will" that asks not to prolong your suffering in case of a terminal illness. These are given consideration by the state. And if you'd like to help out medical science, you're urged to carry a card designating you as an organ donor.

The other inevitable—taxes

As you read above, Florida is among the six states having no inheritance tax. But while there is no tax *per se,* in case part of the estate is subject to the federal law that allows the state to keep a portion, Florida will take it. If not, it would be retained by the federal government anyway so there is no additional burden on the estate.

The state constitution prohibits a state income tax. Amendments have to be approved by voters, which makes it unlikely that such a tax will ever pass. However, during 1987 when new sources of revenue had to be found, publicity was given to the "fairness" of such a tax in that it would fall more heavily on the rich. At least one poll showed a 40% approval over the alternative of an increased sales tax.

The sales tax was raised instead. Prior to 1982 it was 4%; then it was raised to 5%; and in 1987 it went up another penny. There was even an option that allowed counties to tack on an additional 1% for a stated time and stated purpose, and by early the next year ten had taken advantage of this chance. The tax applies to retail sales except food for home consumption, professional services, medicines, and many over-the-counter drugs. For a short while services were taxed, but it proved so unpopular and unwieldly that it was rescinded. The sales tax is the state's primary source of revenue.

In part the crunch is felt by municipalities and county commissioners because of another law written into the constitution. It's called the "homestead exemption," and it states that the first $25,000 value in a person's primary residence is exempt from property taxes. To qualify for the exemption all a homeowner has to do is register his domicile with the county tax office between January 1 and March 1 every year. However, residents who applied previously are mailed an application for renewal. The amount of tax savings varies from location to location, but a ball park figure is $400.

Mobile home owners on rented lots do not qualify, but those on land on which the residents own shares, do. Extra exemptions of $500 of taxes are available to widows and widowers who own homes and for the completely and permanently disabled. Disabled servicemen in the latter category can get a 100 percent exemption. Fully exempt because of their use are such facilities as not-for-profit hospitals and churches.

Localities need to derive a large portion of their income from property taxes, for they are limited because most other sources of taxation are reserved for states and counties. These restrictions lead them to search for whatever other sources of revenue the state permits.

To begin with, they set the property appraisal (current valuation) at what is stated as 100%, but is probably closer to 80%. They tax businesses and utilities, vacant lots, and second homes. Also, any part of your home not classified as the homestead may be subject to a tax on tangible property, which includes such fixtures as utility sheds, garages, and screened porches. They charge for permits and collect fees, and they receive a portion of the state's revenue.

Among one-time taxes are impact fees which many municipalities apply to new housing developments and commercial and industrial concerns to help pay for the new roads, schools, and sewers that are needed. These are going up and up as more funds are required to expand the infrastructure to accommodate growth.

Intangibles, which include taxable investments, but not bank accounts, certificates of deposit, obligations of the United States and of Florida municipalities, and the proceeds of insurance, are taxed by the state at $1 per $1,000 valuation as of December 31st each year. The income is not taxable. The first $20,000 of such property is exempt for a single person and the first $40,000 for a couple.

There are also state documentary taxes, which are set at $.55 per $100 for deeds and at different rates for other documents.

School taxes have increased because of efforts to improve the low standing of the state in educational ranking. Teachers' average salaries, for example, improved from being 36th among the 50 states in the 1981-82 year to 29th in 1986-87, according to the Florida Department of Education. In figures released in January 1988 the state was 49th in the percentage of high school students who went on to graduate. Unfortunately, many tax dollars have to be spent on school buildings to meet the phenomenal growth. Although state-of-the-art features may be incorporated in the new buildings, financing them cuts into many other programs.

In 1987 the voters overwhelmingly approved a state lottery, the proceeds of which were meant for education. It opened a short time later, in January 1988, and the first seven days' sales totaled a record $7.79 for every person in the state. According to a poll of voters, two-thirds said they would buy lottery tickets at the rate of $10 a month.

Taxes and laws are areas in which information becomes quickly outdated. You will need to inquire about current tax rates and any changes in laws when you become a Florida resident. Highly recommended for understanding the legal and financial aspects of Florida retirement is the *Florida Retirees' Handbook,* written by longtime Florida attorney, Elwood Phillips.

Boating, Fishing and Hunting

Boating.   Bring your boat along and transfer your registration or buy a new one in Florida. You'll get more year-round use than you did up North.

The county tax collector is the person to see to register your power boat. You have to prove it's yours, pay the fee, and paint the number on the bow of your boat in contrasting paint with block numerals at least three inches high. If you have bought a used boat, the number already affixed stays with the boat. If you buy a new one, the dealer will probably take care of obtaining your title, paying your initial yearly fee, and stenciling your numerals. You must carry your title certificate on board at all times, and display on the port side a decal indicating the fee has been paid for the year. The fee is renewable every July 1st.

As long as it's not used commercially, your boat can be registered for the following fees:

Less than 12 feet in length	$ 4.25
12 feet but less than 16	8.25

16 feet but less than 26	13.25
26 feet but less than 40	33.25
40 feet but less than 65	53.25

You're going to need a vehicle license tag for your boat trailer, too, don't forget.

Because of the extensive waterways and the mild climate, there are many boats registered in Florida. This means heavy traffic and increases the possibility of accidents. In 1987 there were 107 boating fatalities in the state, leading to the passage of the Vessel Homicide Act, providing penalties of up to five years' imprisonment for careless boat handling that causes another's death.

Novice boaters, especially those going to sea, need to be acquainted with navigational terms and practices, which can be obtained from the U.S. Coast Guard. Appendix V has a handy guide to interpreting the descriptive terms for windspeeds and storm warnings.

Fishing. If you're goin' fishin', while you don't need a license currently to try your luck in the ocean, the legislature has been considering such a requirement. In fresh water residents have to pay $9.00 for the privilege, unless they're under the age of 15 or over 65. To avoid a hassle with the fish and game warden, seniors should carry a permit. Nonresident fees are $12 for ten consecutive days, and $27 for an annual license.

There are two more points to note about fishing licenses. The annual license for residents and nonresidents is for the term beginning June 1st of a year and ending June 30th of the following year. There is a single price for this period with no pro rata charges for part of a year. The other consideration is that to get your first resident license, you must have lived in the state for six months, even if you're over 65. To qualify sooner, you, and your spouse, if you're married, can apply to the clerk of the courts for a certificate of domicile and pay a fee of $9.00. This shows your intention of becoming a permanent resident, and will entitle you to an immediate resident's license.

Ah, retirement! Plenty of time for fishing and enjoying the
grandchildren.

With all the shoreline, lakes, rivers, streams, and canals waiting for them to drop a line, fishermen have come to the right

place. Florida is the bass fishing capital of the world. Annual tournaments are held, including the prestigious one in the Harris chain of lakes at Leesburg every February. Called "Mega-bucks," and sponsored by boating and tackle manufacturers, it paid a record $730,000 in prizes in 1988. Bass isn't the only gamefish, of course, and you're invited, among other contests, to take part in "crappiethons." There are also deep sea fishing contests in many shore communities.

The local papers and the nightly news on television report the best fishing times and which fish are most likely to bite. Salt-water anglers might like to invest in a 112-page guide of 500 fishing holes, species available, best season, and best baits and lures. This handy guide is entitled "Florida's Charted Saltwater Fishin' Holes." Address the Bureau of Maps and Charts, Drawer 5317, Tallahassee, Fl 32301. The guide cost $4.50 post-paid in 1988.

There are, of course, bag limits on your catch.

Hunting.   Hunting in Florida is different from stalking deer through the forests in late fall back home. The seasons and the game vary from year to year. Only common animals such as the fox, raccoon, opossum, and rabbit are usually in season year-round, but you may need your license stamped to indicate that you have complied with special restrictions on methods of hunt-ing. The seasons in which some kind of game may be hunted run from September to April. Included are deer, turkey, quail, waterfowl and wild hogs. Regulations are tricky, and you need to get full information from the sporting goods store or by writ-ing to the Fish and Game Commission, Tallahassee, Fl 32301.

The simplest license a resident can have, a "K" class, costs $12.00 for the same period of June 1st to June 30th that applied to fishing licenses. Once again, residents under 15 or over 65 pay no charges. The same certificate of domicile will waive the requirement of six months' residence. Most out-of-state hunters pay $51.00 for the same privilege. The cost depends on a recip-rocal arrangement between states.

Only animals that are considered a renewable resource may be hunted, and from time to time this classification is changed. Besides, certain quarry and certain types of weapons require additional permits. These are stamps affixed to the regular license. An "MA" stamp, which carries an extra charge, is a permit to hunt in state wildlife management areas. On federal property other stamps are required. Trapping, using bows and arrows, or shooting with antique guns require stamps. As you can see, hunting is strictly regulated.

Last, residents can get a combination hunting and fishing license, designated "AK," for $19.00 a year. If you're 65 years of age, you don't need a license, just proof of age and residency.

Medical care

The prospect for a longer life in Florida, noted earlier in this chapter, is heartening to retirees. Part of this is no doubt due to the less demanding life style; part from the less rigorous climate. At first your body is geared to tolerate cool temperatures, but as you become acclimated, you'll feel chilled by them. Conventional wisdom says your blood thins, but physicians explain that it's because the capillaries that carry your blood move slightly away from the topmost layers of your skin to maintain proper body temperature.

Another contributing factor to a longer life is the increased opportunity to exercise, especially since the exercise seems more like play. Senior citizens can golf year-round, swim possibly eight months of the year, bicycle, hike, and play shuffleboard, boccie, or quoits. Just simple walking is great for your health, and it's very good for your social alertness. Bowling, ping pong, and group exercise programs are among the leading indoor activities. The more strenuous exercises, such as jogging or participating in Senior Olympics games, need clearance from your doctor.

There are exercise programs and weight-control groups in all but the smallest communities in the state. They may be in mobile home park or condo recreation buildings, community sponsored senior citizens' centers, federally funded activities of the Council on Aging, or just among persons with common interests. Some of these organizations choose amusing acronyms for their names like TOPS, Take Off Pounds Sensibly, and BELL, Be Energetic and Live Longer. The upbeat music and the good company make even a diehard relax-o-phile join in the fun.

If you get sick, you will find facilities in Florida are comparable with those elsewhere. The nationwide proportion of physicians per 100,000 of population was 196 and Florida's was 187 in 1986. Per diem hospital costs for in-patients was $440.36. The Florida Association of Homes for the Aging listed 153 members the same year. Hospitals provided close to five beds per 1,000 persons. Special facilities are found in major cities. Most well known are the Shands Teaching Hospital in Gainesville and the Florida branch of the Mayo Clinic in Jacksonville.

The leading causes of deaths in the state among senior citizens, listed in the *Florida Almanac* for 1988-89 are cancer, heart attacks, and strokes.

You need to be extra careful in Florida to protect yourself from too much exposure to the sun. The incidence of skin cancer is high. Whenever you will be outdoors for an extended period of time, wear a hat for protection, and cover the vulnerable areas of your skin with a sun screen that has a rating of 15 or higher. It's also important to wear sunglasses.

Two problems that concern medical services throughout the country also afflict the state. There is the continuing controversy about the high cost of malpractice insurance paid by doctors. In 1988 the legislature held a special session in an effort to find a formula to settle claims against doctors in an equitable manner. They set limits on noneconomic expense awards and made it harder to sue emergency room doctors. They set up a no-fault insurance system for babies who suffer neurological injuries during birth. The governor signed the bill, but neither he nor the legislature nor the doctors and lawyers think it's perfect. Changes are anticipated.

The second problem is the regulation of health maintenance organizations (HMOs). The idea of paying a regular fee for access to whatever health needs you may have sounds good, but the operators of HMOs were breaking new ground, and they had financial obligations they hadn't expected. Quite a few went bankrupt, leaving their clients temporarily without coverage.

The federal government provided support for the families of patients with expensive, long-term illnesses in the passage of the Catastrophic Illness Act of 1988, effective January 1, 1989. Funding is from a surcharge on Medicare deductions. While this is most welcome help for the elderly, it doesn't address the problem of long-term care in a nursing home. Until some relief is found, the unfortunate family whose ability to pay for such care is exhausted has to have the patient cared for under the Medicaid program.

Florida seniors over 65 are covered by Medicare. The state headquarters is at this address: Blue Shield of Florida, Inc., Medicare Part B, P.O. Box 2525, Jacksonville, Fl 32231. There is a special advantage for those enrolled in supplemental coverage by Blue Cross/Blue Shield of Florida, for after the Medicare claim is processed, the supplemental claim is automatically entered. However, you don't have to enroll in Florida Blue Cross. You may have a health plan from your former employment that costs you less or has better coverage. In that case, you or the provider is responsible for sending the claim for residual benefits there directly.

One retired couple in Central Florida, who were enrolled in Medicare and a group plan of an out-of-state supplemental carrier that included "major medical" coverage, paid these amounts for insurance, not including out-of-pocket expenses for deductibles and those services ineligible for coverage:

1984	$1,270
1985	1,365
1986	1,394
1987	1,566
1988	1,772

If you qualify to use a Veterans' Hospital, you will find five of them in the state: Bay Pines (St. Petersburg), Gainesville, Lake City, Miami, and Tampa. Should the sad time come when someone you care for needs to spend time in a mental hospital, there should be one of the seven in the state near you: Arcadia, Avon Park, Chattahoochee, Gainesville, Hollywood, Macclenny, and Tampa.

Retirement homes with medical coverage for their residents are being developed throughout Florida. Before you commit yourself to "lifetime care," read the agreement carefully. Make your family aware of the terms before you sign them, and also get legal advice.

These developments, which are described in the section on assisted living in Chapter 9, have limits on the length of time you can receive certain medical care. They also are partially reimbursed by collecting your Medicare allowances wherever they apply.

Two facts about pharmacies are relevant to senior citizens. First, the state gives a consumer the option of choosing generic prescriptions if the doctor hasn't specifically asked for the brand of medication. Second, pharmacists are permitted to prescribe a limited number of drugs, such as analgesics and topical preparations.

Florida's businesses

The business climate of Florida is important to you even though you're no longer in the work force, for it's a factor in the taxes you pay and in the environment in which you live.

Tourism. As you can probably guess, tourism is the best source of income for the economy of the state, and it's been growing rather than tapering off. The proceeds of this bonanza account for about a quarter of the state budget. Considering the number of residents (12,000,000), it's amazing to learn that the number of visitors has been close to 40,000,000 a year during the 80s.

Miami Beach symbolizes the attractions that make tourism the # 1 business in the state.

Many statistics are collected, both by businesses and the state, in an effort to understand what attracts tourists and how to increase the traffic. Look at these figures for 1986:

State of origin	% of Total Guests
New York	14.7
New Jersey	8.7
Illinois	7.5
Pennsylvania	6.0
California	5.6

Counties Visited	% of Total Guests
Orange, Osceola	26.2
Dade	23.3
Broward	13.8
Palm Beach	9.8
Pinellas	8.2

(Source: *Florida Statistical Abstract*)

The Association of European Airlines reported that in the first nine months of 1987, 7.2 million passengers flew to the U.S., most of them to Florida. Surveys of North American visitors show that more than 96% say they plan to return to the state another time.

Agriculture.   Agriculture is the second greatest source of income, with citrus products the best known. Oranges were the undisputed leading crop until the devastating freezes of December 1983 and January 1985. A measure of how bad these freezes were is seen in Lake County, which once had 125,000 acres under cultivation, and in 1988 had about 20,000.

So much of the acreage that was destroyed has not been replanted. The stick skeletons of dead trees stand desolately behind the "For Sale" signs. Some were pruned of all bearing wood in a fashion known as "staghorning" to save them, and some died as they stood, their branches merely sticks. If you see new shoots at the base of these trees, don't be deceived into thinking they're recovering. They're suckers growing from the rootstock below the graft.

There are several levels of cold that affect the citrus crop. Experts say 27 degrees for four hours is the point at which ice crystals form on fruit; the freezing point is in the low to mid 20s;

and temperatures below 16 degrees for a sustained period can kill the trees.

As a measure of the changes in the production of oranges, consider these figures from the Florida Agricultural Statistical Service:

Peak year, 1980-81	172 million boxes
Recovery, 1986-87	119.7
Estimate, 1987-88	140.

(When growers speak of "boxes," they're talking about 90 pounds, which is 4.5 bushels or 200 to 225 oranges.)

Besides frost damage, citrus can be hurt by a blight called canker. As soon as it has been determined that canker is found in a grove or a nursery, measures are taken to contain the outbreak. Most often this takes the form of destroying the trees. Citrus Mutual researchers say 900,000 trees valued at $100 million are destroyed every year.

In the nurseries citrus shoots are grafted onto rootstock when they are as thick as a pencil. They are planted after two or three years of growth in even rows usually with cuffs of plastic or piled-up earth to protect the young trees. They used to be planted 70 to an acre, or one tree every 25 to 30 feet apart with 25 feet allowed between rows for cultivation and harvesting, but now some growers are planting as many as 175 trees to an acre. The new pattern has been adopted to create a tightly massed growth in order better to resist a freeze. In addition, hardier root stocks have been developed, circulation systems and overhead water jets are used to fight the cold, and, more rarely, heaters are installed.

Florida's soil and climate is best for juice oranges, and indeed, most of the crop ends up as orange juice concentrate. A box makes 1.37 gallons of concentrate, or about 30 6-oz. cans. After the juice is extracted, the orange pulp and "molasses" are served as cattle feed. Even the seeds are made into oil. Whatever is not used for eating by hand or drinking could be turned into citrus wines, marmalades, jellies, candies, or industrial alcohol.

The first orange blossoms open in March, and the air is sweet with their smell. White boxes of beehives line the edges of the groves, their residents eager to perform their service in the food chain. The citrus honey taken from them has a distinctive flavor, and makes a nice souvenir for your Northern guests.

During the harvesting season, from early December to late April, processing of juice oranges takes place up to 24 hours a day. Trucks with steel mesh sides carry 22.5 tons of oranges on each trip to the processing plant, where their cargo is unloaded by tilting a ramp that holds the truck to spill the contents out onto conveyor belts. After that they are scrubbed, pierced, and pressed; the juice is "baked" to concentrate it and the by-products are recovered. Juice which is not concentrated is pasteurized.

With the advances in growing citrus developed through research and the demand for the products, economists have pre-dicted that by the year 2000 the crop should run about 80% of pre-freeze growth. The citrus belt, however, will be farther south.

You might want to compare Florida's acreage under cultiva-tion with that of the competition ('85-'86 season):

Oranges	Grapefruit	State
367,600	105,100	Florida
10,900	7,100	Arizona
174,700	20,900	California
11,400	19,100	Texas

(Source: *Florida Statistical Abstract*)

Another important product is sugar, found in a belt beginning at Lake Okeechobee. Florida's sugar cane crop, which is ready for harvest early in October, surpassed Hawaii's to become first in the United States in 1982. It has stayed in first place. In 1985 the crop amounted to 12,615,000 tons of raw sugar. Like many agricultural products in the country, it is subsidized. In Decem-ber of 1987 the federal government supported the price at $.218 per pound. At the time the world market price per pound was

$.09. Sugar was stockpiling in the warehouses, and protests from consumer groups were mounting.

The muck farms in south Florida that were once part of the Everglades system produce many winter vegetables for the Northeast. They grow in an other-world setting that produces as many as three crops a year. Across the flat land are row after row of punched plastic strips paralleled by trenches. In each punched-out hole is a seedling sprouting or a plant flourishing in the rich soil and artificial irrigation. Strange and startling, isn't it? The land was once covered by a river of water, flowing over lush grass, and now it has to have water fed to it in pipes.

The other leading agricultural products are field and sweet corn, wheat, cotton, potatoes, tobacco, cattle, and swine. Florida's strawberries, which represent 17% of the nation's fresh berries, ripen naturally in the period between December and April to cheer the appetites of winter-weary Northerners, and blueberries are at their peak in April. In the summer exotic fruits like mangoes and avocados go to market.

A newcomer to the rolling hills of central Florida may take over some abandoned land that once was home to orange groves: grapes. There were five wineries in Florida in 1988. The largest of these was Lafayette Vineyards, which first opened in 1982 in Tallahassee. Begun after encouraging results in research showed that quality grapes could flourish in the sandy soil and warm climate of Florida, the winery was visited by 35,000 tourists in 1987 and sold 100,000 bottles of 20 different varieties of wine. The wines achieved recognition by winning 26 awards in local and international competition in the first years.

Lafayette Vineyards purchased 113 acres to plant, and set aside space for a winery and visitor's center on Highway 27 just north of the city of Clermont. The wines will be grown mostly from native muscadine varieties, but drier wines will be made from cold-resistant hybrids such as Stover, Suwannee, and Blanc du Bois.

Minerals.   There are minerals of commercial value in Florida. Sand and gravel are first, followed by phosphate, the second largest concentration in the world. Limestone is harvested primarily in Florida Bay, which lies between the mainland and the Keys, and also in the Panhandle. Found in a smooth-textured variety and one called coquina, which is loosely formed with inclusions of marine shells, limestone is used for building or crushed for roadbeds. Cement and uranium are also mined.

Phosphate mining, while important to the making of fertilizers, has the potential for a bad side effect. Where the deposits occur or where abandoned mines lie, a cancer-causing gas called radon is disseminated. The gas is the end product of the decay of the uranium content of phosphate into radium and eventually into radon. Some homes in several critical areas, mainly in Alachua, Marion, and Polk Counties, have shown intolerably high levels of the gas. Dangerous concentrations of radon are not confined to Florida, but are found in many states. Kits for checking radon levels are widely available throughout the state.

Fuller's earth, zircon, and peat are in high concentration in different areas, and kaolin, a type of clay used for fine china, is found in commercially usable amounts. Some unusual minerals are extracted from beach sands.

Industries.   Among the oldest industries in the state are the harvesting of pulpwood and the extraction of naval stores from pine trees. Although the size of its petroleum deposits can't compete with those of the major oil-producing states, Florida does have oil wells in Santa Rosa County and possibly also has offshore deposits.

What the state seeks is the kind of industry courted by others: nonpolluting manufacturing plants, corporate headquarters, research and development facilities, publishing houses, high-tech companies, and producers of pharmaceuticals.

Commerce.   Prospective commercial businesses are interested in the per capita income of the residents. According to the U.S. Department of Commerce, in 1986 this was $14,281, up from $9,246 in 1980. In total personal income among the 50 states Florida was 6th in rank.

Companies are attracted to the state because of the favorable business climate. In a 1983 report it placed first among the 50 states with a score of 79.4. The categories used in determining relative climates were: fiscal policies, state-regulated employment costs, labor costs, the availability and quality of workers, and accessible resources.

The principal ports are Tampa Harbor, Jacksonville, Port Everglades, Port Canaveral, Manatee County (Bradenton area), and Palm Beach.

Bringing money into the state, especially to the nearby cities, are the major military bases. These are the Pensacola Naval Air Station, Eglin Air Force Base (Tallahassee), the Orlando Naval Training Center, MacDill Air Force Base (Tampa), Homestead Air Force Base, and the Mayport Naval Station (Jacksonville).

Municipalities struggling with the problems of crowded roads have set up car-pooling incentives, subsidized commuter buses, and provided park-and-ride areas. It isn't possible to dig subways anywhere in the state, and overhead people-movers, that are being investigated, are all costly. After much discussion, the first steps are being taken to build a bullet train to link Tampa, Orlando, and Miami.

The principal population centers as of April 1986, according to the 1987 *Florida Statistical Abstract* are:

Jacksonville	609,614
Miami	371,975
Tampa	278,755
St. Petersburg	243,090
Fort Lauderdale	151,048

However, when the entire metropolitan areas are considered, the figures are:

Jacksonville	850,149
Tampa–St. Petersburg–Clearwater	1,910,023
Miami–Hialeah	1,776,099
Ft. Lauderdale–Hollywood–Pompano Beach	1,149,200

Regional banks have taken over a big share of the banking in the state, but local commercial banks and savings and loans are still common. Florida has not experienced the high rate of failures and mergers that have occurred in different sections of the country, but some institutions are at risk and have been kept from folding by the FDIC and the FSLIC. Rates of return on money market funds and certificates of deposit are slightly better than the national average.

Competition among the banks for the savings deposits of senior citizens has led to some special perquisites. By meeting certain criteria, for instance having three types of accounts in a given bank, seniors are provided with a number of free services. These vary from bank to bank, but are likely to include: free personal checks; interest on checking accounts, and no monthly fees if the balance stays at a certain level; free traveler's checks, money orders, and cashier's checks; free VISA or MasterCard; free notary public and limited photocopy service; $100,000 common carrier life insurance; and a 24-hour automatic teller card.

At least 40,600 families don't have to worry about saving pennies. That's the number of millionaires in the state, according to the U.S. Department of Commerce figures in 1988. Florida was No. 2 in this elite category.

Criminal activities

The most law-abiding citizens are the retired. In areas where they are in the greatest concentration, the crime rates are the lowest. They are, however, while not the perpetrators, often the victims of crime. Crime is not spread evenly throughout the state. It occurs in pockets, notably in South Florida and in the largest cities. In urban areas vulnerability increases, but outlying districts aren't safe, either.

In 1987, according to the Florida Department of Law Enforcement (FDLE), more than a million serious crimes were reported. In the category of "serious crimes" are murder, forcible rape, robbery, aggravated assault, burglary, larceny, and the theft of motor vehicles. To put this into perspective, think of a residential burglary taking place every two minutes somewhere in the state.

These figures represented a 6.3% increase over the previous year. The growing rate was blamed primarily on two factors: the drug trade and the burgeoning population. The Commissioner of the FDLE reported a correlation between the 33% rise in arrests concerned with cocaine use and the rise in crimes involving property. He also reported that homegrown marijuana flourishes in all 67 counties. The growth in population means more criminals enter the state and more victims suffer as their targets.

Certainly Florida cannot be proud of its first place in overall crime rate among the states. In early 1988 three of every thousand persons was in prison, the fourth highest population of inmates, again according to the FDLE. The cost of keeping them there is close to $400 million a year.

Another measurement used by police is counting the number of crimes per 100,000 of population. The U.S. average in 1985 was 5,207. Florida was first with 7,574 and Arizona second with 7,116. The District of Columbia, not a state, topped them both with 8,007 crimes per 100,000.

Early release of prisoners and alternatives, such as house arrest, community service, and probation, are devices used whenever possible to keep the number of inmates close to the capacity of the prisons, but new detention centers have to be built just to keep up with growth.

The FDLE reported 6,545 murders in the five years from 1982 through 1986. Of these 4,491, or 68%, were solved.

In 1987 the state legislature enacted a handgun law that is among the most liberal in the land. Almost any adult can get a permit to carry a concealed weapon. Statistics are not out yet on whether this will contribute to the number of crimes. The 1988 legislature eased off a bit by allowing counties by local option to require a three-day cooling off period before a gun is sold.

There is no doubt of the correlation between the high crime rate and drug trafficking. Florida's geographic situation makes it a most attractive dropping-off point for illegal narcotics.

After all those laws and statistics and detailed information have been digested, you'll be happy to read about some places to relax. Try Chapter 4, A Permanent Vacation, for suggestions on having fun.

4. A Permanent Vacation

With freedom from work, with year-round sunshine and an incredible stretch of beaches, with the gift of natural beauty and the imaginative man-made entertainment, life in Florida can be a permanent vacation.

What's your pleasure: natural parks, outdoor sports, historic places, museums, camping, cultural activities, boating, dining out, races, shopping? You've come to the right state.

As a general rule, the prices are less than they would be back home for comparable entertainment, particularly if you lived near a large city. There are luxury accommodations if you wish, beautiful hotels and sumptuous meals, cruises, lavishly tailored golf courses, and seaside villas. There are inexpensive places to live and free places to visit. A collection of hundreds of "freebies" is published by the state, and while they're free, they're not "cheap." You go to them to enjoy or enlighten yourself, not just to save money. For your copy write to the Florida Division of Tourism, Office of Visitor Inquiry, 126 Van Buren Street, Tallahassee, Fl 32301.

Enjoying nature

Florida's state parks, which cover 260,000 acres, are among the finest in the nation. In 1986 over 14 million people visited

Most places in Florida are 40 miles or
less from a beach.

them. The most favored (those having over 1/2 million visitors) were Sebastian Inlet between Melbourne and Vero Beach, St. Joseph Peninsula near Port St. Joe, Anastasia on the St. Johns River, Cape Florida in Dade and Glades Counties, Honeymoon Island in Pinellas County, Lake Talquin near Tallahassee, and Lloyd Beach near Fort Lauderdale. In the same year 11.5 million visited the national parks. Their favorites were beaches at Cape Canaveral and at Gulf Island National Seashore near Pensacola, 1.1 million and 7.6 million visitors respectively.

The state facilities come with a great variety of offerings: lakes, beaches, springs, woods, nature trails, horseback riding, picnicking, boat and canoe rentals, snorkeling, scuba diving, coral reefs, caverns, museums, historical monuments, botanical preserves, and animal and bird refuges. Besides diversity, they offer bargain prices. Where there's an entrance fee, it's nominal. Camping fees are also inexpensive, but you must reserve ahead at the specific park you wish to visit. Consult the phone book and call or write the park ranger.

The Department of Natural Resources is trying to do a balancing act in its treatment of the recreational facilities. It has been attempting to stretch its appropriation money by raising fees and adding commercial enterprises, such as concessions, lodging, and rentals, to the parks. The proposed policy has caused outcries by people living near the parks, by businesses fearing loss of income from the competition, and by environmentalists worried about overuse.

In Appendix I is a list of the 104 state facilities, four state forests, and the national parks and forests. They're coded to show what kind of park each is and whether there are trailer and tent camping spaces or vacation cottages available. If you'd like further information, you can write to the Florida Department of Natural Resources, Education and Information Office, 3900 Commonwealth Blvd., Tallahassee, Fl 32304.

Visiting Florida's outstanding natural springs is one of the most fascinating of outdoor activities. There are more than 60 large ones and countless small ones throughout the state. Their combined output is estimated at seven billion gallons a day. You may be interested in the scale on which the output of these springs is measured. Those of the first magnitude discharge 100 cubic feet or more *per second*. Twenty-seven of Florida's springs are so classified. The second magnitude output is from 10 to 100 cubic feet per second, and the third is 10 or less. The water comes from the aquifer, about which there is more information in Chapter 10, entitled "The Endangered Environment."

The pure, natural spring water is good for drinking, swimming, fishing, or just sightseeing. Generally it's warm, from 68 degrees to somewhere in the 80s. Many of the springs are in developed areas with picnic sites or other amenities. A list of the location and output of 26 of the major springs is given in Appendix III, but since they're found in 46 of Florida's 67 counties, you might find the nearest one by consulting the chamber of commerce in your town. For even more information, you can purchase a book from the Department of Natural Resources, Bureau of Geology, Division of Interior Resources, Tallahassee, Fl 32304.

Interested volunteers are building a hiking trail to run 1,300 miles when complete. So far, several segments totaling 950 miles have been opened. The longest of these runs from the national forests to the Suwannee River. The winding trail is marked by blazes, which are "easy" to follow. If you try to hike the trail, be sure you have some training as a woodsman, for you will face insects and possible snakebite besides the ruggedness of outdoor life. Take adequate signaling equipment in case you get lost.

Thirty-five of Florida's rivers and creeks have canoe trails. If you'd like more information, a map and a pamphlet are available from the Department of Natural Resources, Tallahassee, Fl 32301.

Spectator sports

If you rooted for the Boston Celtics or the Pittsburgh Pirates or the Minnesota Vikings or Notre Dame or Ohio State, you can still follow your favorites on television, but you'll soon learn to root for your new home teams as well.

In the NFL these are, of course, the Miami Dolphins and the Tampa Bay Buccaneers. You'll soon recognize the college teams from the many bumper stickers touting the Gators of the University of Florida, the Seminoles of Florida State, the Rattlers of Florida A&M, and the Hurricanes of the University of Miami. Recently some of these have had eminently respectable records in college play. Football fans can also attend the invitational games at the end of the college season at the Orange Bowl (or its replacement) in Miami, the Gator Bowl in Jacksonville, and the Citrus Bowl in Orlando. And early in the 90s Tampa will host the Super Bowl.

In the 1989-90 pro basketball season the Miami Heat and the Orlando Magic teams take to the courts for their first games in the NBA expansion program.

In baseball, Florida hasn't yet landed a pro team. Jacksonville has been pursuing this dream, but St. Petersburg jumped the gun and is building a beautiful stadium. The 1988 legislature gave the city a boost by providing a kitty of $30 million to lure the Chicago White Sox, but the loyal fans back home gave them an offer they couldn't refuse.

Meanwhile, Florida is host to most of the major league players for spring training from February to April. Except for eight teams that train in the Cactus League in Arizona and California, Florida is the spring home of both leagues.

You can find an inexpensive seat at these practice games and see your favorite players close up. In the informality of preseason you have a better chance to talk personally to some of the players. You can get a preview of the performance of the team's rookies. You can yell yourself hoarse, have a hot dog and a cool drink, and watch a good game.

From time to time teams leave one training field for another. If this happens, or if you want a schedule of spring games, you can get one from the Division of Tourism. With that understanding, these are the teams' homes in the Grapefruit League in 1988:

American League

Minnesota Twins, Orlando, Tinker Field
Texas Rangers, Port Charlotte, County Stadium
Kansas City Royals, Haines City, Boardwalk and
　　Baseball
New York Yankees, Fort Lauderdale, City Stadium
Toronto Blue Jays, Dunedin, Grant Field
Boston Red Sox, Winter Haven, Chain O'Lakes Park
Detroit Tigers, Lakeland, Marchant Stadium
Baltimore Orioles, Miami, Bobby Maduro Stadium
Chicago White Sox, Sarasota, Payne Park (replacement
　　due in 1989)

National League

Cincinnati Reds, Plant City, Plant City Stadium

St. Louis Cardinals, St. Petersburg, Al Lang Stadium
Montreal Expos, West Palm Beach, Municipal Stadium
Los Angeles Dodgers, Vero Beach, Holman Stadium
Houston Astros, Kissimmee, Osceola County Stadium
New York Mets, Port St. Lucie, County Sports Complex
Philadelphia Phillies, Clearwater, Jack Russell Stadium
Atlanta Braves, West Palm Beach, Municipal Stadium
Pittsburgh Pirates, Bradenton, McKetchnie Field

Cultural interests

Music and performing arts.   If you're a lover of cultural affairs, you'll find regional symphony orchestras and chamber music groups of excellent caliber. These are cities that currently have symphony orchestras: Gainesville, Melbourne, Ft. Lauderdale, Hollywood, Hallandale, Sarasota, Venice, Naples, Miami, Jacksonville, Tampa, Pensacola, Fort Myers, Tallahassee, Okaloosa, Orlando, Palm Beach, Clearwater, and Lakeland.

Repertory and civic theaters and straw hat players offer presentations in most cities, and a winter season of Broadway shows is offered in the major ones. The state theater, Asolo, in Sarasota is a prestigious performing arts center. Balletomanes can enjoy local talent and touring groups. Civic centers and large auditoriums, like Tupperware in Kissimmee and the Ruth Eckerd Theater in Clearwater, feature both popular and world-famous performers during the cooler months. Ballroom dancing to live music is found in many locations because it's of special interest to nostalgic seniors. If there's none in your community, watch for locally sponsored dances. The mecca for ballroom dancing is the Coliseum in St. Petersburg.

Museums.   The Ringling Museum in Sarasota has been hailed as the finest museum south of the District of Columbia. It has a collection of such masters as Rubens, Hals, Tintoretto, Van Dyke, Rembrandt, Titian, Velasquez, Murillo, Goya, Reynolds, and Gainsborough. Visitors can also tour the Ringling Mansion and the interesting and informative museum of the circus. The complex is likewise home to the state theater, Asolo, and tours are given there at hours when the building is free.

St. Petersburg has a museum devoted to the works of Salvador Dali. Miami has the Bass Museum of Art, and Tallahassee has the Florida State Art Gallery and the Museum of Florida History. West Palm Beach has the Norton Gallery of Art. Jacksonville has two art museums, and Gainesville is home to the University Art Museum and the Florida State Museum.

A museum of a different type is in Fort Myers. It's Edison's Winter Home, with exhibits and memorabilia and beautiful gardens. Others devoted to specific people are the Ernest Hemingway Home in Key West, the Stephen Foster State Center in White Springs, and the Marjorie Kinnan Rawlings House near Gainesville. If you're an Elvis Presley fan, there are more than 300 mementos on display in Orlando. Vizcaya, an Italian Renaissance palace in Miami, is a monument to millionaire John Deering.

Graphic and sculptural art works are on display at the Maitland Art Center, at the Miami Design Preservation Center, at the Museum of Fine Art in St. Petersburg, at the Flagler Art Gallery in West Palm Beach, at the unique Coral Castle in Homestead, and at many other local museums and art shows.

Noteworthy for scientific exhibits are the Florida State Museum in Gainesville, the Orlando Science Center, the Museum of Arts and Sciences in Daytona Beach, the Museum of Science and Industry in Tampa, and the Science Museum and Planetarium in West Palm Beach. Industry is depicted in the Transportation Museum in Pensacola and the Gold Coast Railroad Museum in Miami, among others.

Back to school. If you'd like to polish up your skills, dabble with practical or graphic arts, or finish getting your degree, you'll find many opportunities in Florida. Tuition is low for Florida residents taking credit in state universities, and in many of the community colleges senior citizens may study free if there's room left in a course after paying students have signed up.

There are 28 community colleges scattered around the state in the most populous locations. They're listed in Appendix II at the end of this book. There are more than 50 private colleges. The best known of these are the University of Miami; Stetson University in the city of DeLand; Tampa University; Bethune-Cookman, a Black college at Daytona Beach; and Florida Southern College in Lakeland. The last of these is worth a visit just to see its buildings, which were designed by Frank Lloyd Wright. Among the private colleges are at least a dozen with ties to churches or emphasis on Christian education.

The state universities are located on different campuses in all parts of the state. The main campus is in Gainesville, where it was founded in 1853. The second oldest is Florida A&M, Tallahassee, 1887. The remaining were all founded in the 60s and 70s to keep pace with population growth.

Here is a list of their locations and the enrollment in 1986, figures taken from Alan Morris' *Florida Handbook:*

University of Florida, Gainesville, 35,171
Florida State, Tallahassee, 23,548
Florida A&M, Tallahassee, 5,077
U. South Florida, Tampa/St. Petersburg, 28,661
Florida Atlantic, Boca Raton, 10,232
U. West Florida, Pensacola, 6,228
U. Central Florida, Orlando, 16,575
Florida International, Miami, 16,258
U. North Florida, Jacksonville, 6,699.

Attractions

The well-known attractions that account for the most tourists' visits are found in Central Florida. They draw 25% of all tourists that come to the state. Although many of these or their predecessors were in business before the Disney era, there is little question that the presence of the Mouse has spawned most of the lesser attractions that have grown up in the area. Disney is still growing in a manner that may crowd out all major competitors. The complex already comprises the Magic Kingdom, EPCOT,

Adventure Island, River Country, World Village, Typhoon Lagoon, resort hotels, and the MGM studio/tour section due to open in April of 1989.

The main attractions in the area are: Walt Disney's Magic Kingdom, a child-oriented theme park near Orlando; EPCOT Center, a technical and travel theme park near Orlando; Sea World, marine shows and exhibits near Orlando; Cypress Gardens, ornamental gardens, rides, shows, and a zoo, in Winter Haven; Boardwalk and Baseball, theme park and sports center, in Haines City; Silver Springs, shows, boat rides, and a collection of classic cars, near Ocala.

Movie Corporation of America is building a complex (similar to the one by MGM mentioned above) that will produce motion pictures and TV shows and offer tours to the public on U.S. 192, the gateway to Disney's properties. It is set to open in December of 1989.

Forty miles to the east of Orlando is Kennedy Space Center, where NASA launches its shuttles and rockets. Besides the spectacle of a firing, visitors are offered tours, exhibits, and shows. The nearest city is Titusville, in the East Central Region.

The Western Region has a principal attraction in Busch Gardens, located in Tampa. Its theme is the "Dark Continent," and it has shows and uncaged wildlife. Two popular lesser attractions are at springs: Weeki Wachee near Brooksville and Homosassa Springs in Homosassa. Near the Everglades are air boat tours, and in Naples an African Safari.

In the Southeast, Parrot Jungle, Miami Seaquarium with marine shows and exhibits, and Lion Country Safari with a tour, boat cruise, and amusements are the main family attractions. The Southeast Region hosts the most foreign visitors, who enter through Miami. Peak times for tourists there are in the winter and the summer.

There are special advantages to Florida residents for the major attractions. Annual and seasonal passes are offered; for example, the Walt Disney Corporation issues three-season passes to the World and EPCOT at $65 per person (1988 prices) for

Take off and visit the launching pad at Kennedy Space Center,
America's stairway to the stars.

unlimited entrances during January, May, and September, the
"slow" months. Annual passes are also available for $165. Har-
court Brace Jovanovich, which operates Cypress Gardens, Sea
World, and Boardwalk and Baseball, sells annual passes good
at all three attractions for $55. Not only are the prices good, but
purchasers can go to the parks at times when there are no long
lines.

Boat rides and cruises.   Almost every major city on the
coast has a company that offers you a cruise of its bay or waterways. The port cities of Canaveral and Tampa are home to one-

day cruises called SeaEscape, which offer two shipboard self-serve meals and a chance to gamble while they putter around outside the statutory limits. Several cities, Daytona Beach and Sanford for example, have short cruises with dinner, dancing, and entertainment. Overnight trips by boat leave from Fort Myers, traveling from the Gulf to the Atlantic, passing through Lake Okeechobee, and finishing at Fort Pierce.

Another novel opportunity is provided by a houseboat rental company that operates on the St. Johns River. The nearest city to the facility is DeLand. The houseboats come in sizes for occupancy by two to ten persons. A refrigerator, sink, range, single head and shower, pull-out beds, table, chairs, and simple dinnerware are provided. Operating the boat doesn't require more than average skill, and a chart shows the contours of the river bottom, the docking facilities, and the service stations and restaurants on shore. Other companies offer rentals on Key Largo, Sebastian Inlet, and the Suwannee River.

Tampa and Miami are the main ports for longer trips to the Caribbean and to Mexican resort cities. Also, international cruises leave from Miami. Among the most popular of these are visits to Mexico, ports in the Mediterranean, through the Panama Canal to the West Coast, and around South America.

Water Parks.   This relatively new type of park appeals mostly to children and young folks who don't mind getting a thorough soaking and who delight in the thrill of plunging down a long waterslide. If it's not your style, you may some day be dragged there by an insistent grandchild and discover it's a whole new idea of having fun.

Besides Walt Disney World's Typhoon Lagoon, Wet and Wild, covering 25 acres, is also in the Orlando area. In Tampa there's Adventure Island and in Brooksville Buccaneer Bay. Wild Waters is next door to Silver Springs near Ocala.

Gardens.   Flower lovers can discover many exotic plants growing outdoors in cultured beauty in the gardens of Florida. That's where it got its name, remember? A sampling of them follows:

Maclay Gardens near Tallahassee
Fairchild Gardens in Miami
Bok Tower Gardens near Lake Wales
The gardens of EPCOT
Sunken Gardens in St. Petersburg
Washington Oaks Gardens, Marineland
Sugar Mills Gardens, Port Orange
Leu and Mead Botanical Gardens, Orlando
Ravine Gardens, Palatka
Eden, Point Washington
Caribbean Gardens, Naples
Everglades Wonder Gardens, Bonita Springs
Marie Selby Botanical Gardens, Sarasota
Jungle Gardens, Sarasota
Tiki Gardens, Indian Rocks Beach
Morikami Japanese Gardens, Delray Beach
Orchid Jungle, Miami
Cypress Gardens, Winter Haven
Slocum Water Gardens, Winter Haven
Parrot Jungle, Miami

Festivals.   There are so many annual festivals in the Sunshine State, there must be one for every interest. The following is by no means a complete list; it's just a sampling. Since the dates change every year and new celebrations are added, you'd be well advised to watch your local papers for details. In case your tastes are so eclectic you like to attend festivals wherever they are, you can write to the Division of Tourism for their current list.

Reenactment of the Civil War battle of Olustee,
    every February since 1977
The Sunshine State Games and the Golden Age
    Games, "Olympic"-type competitions
Florida Classic Safari, a bike tour
Miami-Bahamas Goombay, ethnic fiesta

> Kissimmee Boat-a-cade, a 600-mile trip by private
> boats on the Kissimmee River and Lake
> Okeechobee, with activities along the way
> "Cross and Sword," the official state play, held in
> the spring near St. Augustine
> The St. Johns River Festival, boats and fishing and
> food and fun
> Strawberry Festival, a date in March at Plant City
> Silver Spurs Rodeo, at cattle country headquarters
> in Kissimmee
> Gasparilla "Pirate Invasion," February in Tampa
> Battle of the high school bands, St. Petersburg
> Bluegrass Festival, Arcadia
> Blue Angels Air Show, Pensacola
> Indian Art Festival, Miami.

A world of choices

There are so many places to go and things to do, the lists above can't begin to cover them all. The variety is great and the trouble you take to get there is almost always worthwhile.

The Tupperware World Headquarters in Kissimmee has an interesting tour and gets first-class entertainers in its auditorium. At Tarpon Springs you can watch sponge divers at work and enjoy the brush with Greek culture. You can go turtle watching at Melbourne Beach or Jensen Beach. You can attend the Black Hills Passion Play during Lent each year. It has been held in Lake Wales ever since 1951.

At the Bok Tower Gardens, also near Lake Wales, you can enjoy the carillon and the tower of pink coquina stone and Georgia marble. You can smile knowingly when you read the plaque on an overlook that says it's the highest point in the state because you know the facts about the three claims to this distinction:

> Citrus Tower, Clermont: 317' elevation with a 226'
> tower—543'
> Walton Mountain: 345' natural elevation

Bok Gardens: 324′ elevation with a 255′ tower—579′.

At least once you should drive down the Causeway to Key West, and while you're there take a conch tour and watch the famous sunset. That was the port used by Mel Fisher to bring up the treasure of the ship *Nuestra Senora de Atocha*. Put the Everglades on your must-see list. You can combine it with the trip to the Keys. Best place to enter is at Florida City. Platforms will take you safely to fine overlooks on the wetlands, and a guidebook from the ranger station will help you enjoy the trip. While you're packing, don't forget the insect repellent.

There are alligator farms and serpentariums, zoos, and bird refuges. There are dinner-with-entertainment shows like King Henry's Feast and Mardi Gras, and Medieval Times. There are a wax museum and a replica of HMS Bounty in St. Petersburg. There are glass bottom boat rides on Islamorada Key and at Silver Springs, and there's snorkeling at John Pennekamp Coral Reef State Park.

Near home

You don't need to go far from home to have a good time. In your locality are plenty of activities you can enjoy all year long: golf, tennis, fishing, running, hiking, bicycling, boating, shuffleboard, visiting flea markets, movie-going, art exhibits, group exercise, bingo, sunbathing, church programs, bird-watching, circuses, volunteer work, reading, playing cards, amateur dramatics, joining a chorus or musical group, shopping, and pot luck dinners, to name a few.

There are seasonal activities, too: horse and dog racing, auto races, jai alai, regattas, festivals, foot races and field meets, bike safaris, rodeo, and college and professional sports.

If you're civic-minded, your services are in demand by many worthwhile organizations. You can join the volunteers who teach reading in the literacy program. The local hospital and the library will welcome your services. Churches can always use willing hands, and if you live in a community with a clubhouse, you can find plenty to do in the group activities. Fund raisers for

There are so many golf courses for year-round play that you can almost guarantee one within range of two drivers and a pitching wedge.

the arts, for charity, and for causes you support can all use your help. You might qualify as a teacher's aide. You can even bag groceries in a local supermarket for a limited number of hours, enjoy meeting the shoppers, and get paid, as well.

It's time after all that fun to get down to business. There's a new home to be found. You have some choices that may not have occurred to you: mobile homes, condominiums, cooperatives, single site-built homes or those in a subdivision, congregate living facilities, and nursing homes.

5. *The Mobile Home Option*

A very popular type of home among Florida retirees is the mobile home. It's inexpensive considering the amenities it offers, and it's usually situated in an "adult" park where the neighbors are likely to be in the same age group as the new buyer.

Before you succumb to the lure of the beautiful new models or the ideal surroundings of the park, please read the pros and cons in this chapter and the next.

What is a mobile home?

A mobile home is a complete home built in a factory, hauled to the lot on which it is to be erected, fastened down, landscaped, and hooked to utility lines.

About 35 years ago these homes were called trailers, came eight feet wide, and were used as homes only in poor neighborhoods or as summer homes in the mountains. They retained their wheels and looked more like a boxcar than a home.

Any resemblance between the early models and the homes today is purely evolutionary. Nowadays the single homes are 12

The kitchen and family room of a modern mobile home. Note the smart details, such as the island range, double sink, wood-finished cabinets, ceiling fan.

Courtesy, Manufactured Home News

or 14 feet wide, and the doublewide homes are 24, 26, or 28, and in the case of triplewides even 40 feet wide. They range in length from 30 to 70 feet. More luxuries are being added every year, as a visit to the display models at a factory, at a manufactured housing show, or in a park being developed will show.

Not only are the newer homes state-of-the-art, but the more costly ones in the first class parks can be so altered in their exteriors—with partial foundations, brick or stone facing, and added garages and Florida rooms—that it's hard to tell them from a single family site-built house. Even the price tags are beginning to resemble each other. After you have added the options you want, a deluxe model could cost $70,000—and even $100,000 is not unheard of.

They're not really mobile any more except on their way from the factory. Once a home is settled on a plot of ground and mounted on supports, it can be moved only by professionals at a cost in double-digit thousands and at a risk of damage to the home.

In construction, mobile homes must conform to U.S. government standards and must be so labeled. Nationwide, they are big business. There are over 200 firms building them and approximately 10,000 retailers selling them. In 1986 Florida was first in the sale of new mobile homes with a total of 24,877, more than 10% of those sold in the U.S, according to the Department of Commerce. The Florida Department of Highway Safety and Motor Vehicles reported more than half a million tags were issued as required by law to mobile homes on rental lots in the 1985-86 fiscal year. This does not include the mobile homes on single lots nor the ones in resident-owned parks.

There are differences between mobile homes and modular housing. Both are made in sections with plumbing, heating, and electrical systems installed. Basically, the mobile home, complete with roof and floor, is moved from the factory on a set of wheels, while the modular units are moved on a flatbed truck. The modular home is put on a foundation, while the mobile home has its foundation as an integral part, and needs only to be mounted on supports. These differences are important, however, for a modular home is treated like a site-built house and must conform to local building codes, while the mobile home is built in accordance with the standards of the federal government's Housing and Urban Development Office.

Why should you buy one?

There are many reasons for buying a mobile home, but none is perhaps so important as the cost. While 2/2 (2-bedroom, 2-bath) and 3/2 new homes sell anywhere from the $60s to the $130s, basic mobile homes of comparable size cost from the $20s to the $60s. The wholesale cost of the homes is much lower, but you will have to pay the retail price. Sometimes a buyer can get a bargain on a closeout of a model at the end of a year. Included in the final price are the costs of installation, the state sales tax, and the markup by the park owner.

After the low cost, the priority of reasons for buying a mobile home varies from person to person. The friendly atmosphere of a neighborhood of other retired persons in a mobile home community ranks high among the reasons for buying one. The communities nearly always have a clubhouse for group activities, a swimming pool, and facilities for recreational games such as shuffleboard.

Then there are personal reasons. You have old friends nearby; you are a widow or widower who can't handle the "big house" back home; you want to get away from Northern winters for good; or you'd like an inexpensive winter home.

Since most of the mobile homes come complete with wall-to-wall carpeting, finished kitchens and baths, built-in hutches, ample closets, all major appliances except washer and dryer, draperies, many convenient electrical outlets, and decorator-designed colors, they don't require large expenditures to make them livable. They also have a minimum upkeep and the layout is designed for efficiency. There's usually no delay in delivery to inconvenience the buyer.

Furthermore, you may never need another home, for according to the Federation of Mobile Home Owners of Florida the life of a mobile home is between 30 and 40 years.

One survey of mobile home owners found three major reasons given for their choice: economy of purchase, ownership rather than rental, and low maintenance.

Special features

There are changing styles in homes, just as there are fashions in clothes. One builder adds a new gadget or designs a special feature, and it catches on. So it is with mobile homes. The amenities in the more expensive 1988 models included popular features like paddle fans, double walk-in closets in master bedrooms, Roman tubs, wet bars, family rooms, Jenn-air grills,

Exterior finish of a mobile home model has a site-built look. Notice the landscaping, the many windows, and the siding.

Courtesy, Manufactured Home News

double ovens, "volume" ceilings, fireplaces, breakfast rooms, skylights, dry wall construction, and Florida rooms. (A Florida room is an enclosed lanai or sun porch sometimes structurally integrated with the house.) What will the next features be? Perhaps cleaning systems and media rooms and computer control centers and bidets.

Besides looking good, your home has to function well. Usually a heating system combined with an air conditioner is fastened to the rear of the mobile home and feeds into ducts that vent either through the floor or the ceiling of the rooms. It's a matter of personal choice which you like best, but most people prefer the ceiling vents.

The electric control panel may be set into an interior wall or into an enclosed space on the exterior. If you don't choose to upgrade the capacity, you'll normally be provided with 150 amperes. The hot water tank may hold 30 gallons unless you request more. Adequate lighting fixtures and wall outlets are usually found throughout.

Some items are required by law, either by HUD specifications or by state law. HUD requires the label (usually found in a closet) showing compliance with their regulations. For example, in the snow-free states the roof must have a load potential of 20 pounds per square foot, and hurricane-resistive requirements are 25 p.s.f. horizontal and 15 p.s.f. uplift. Minimum standards for insulation of walls, ceilings, roofs, and flooring must be met, but are occasionally exceeded by manufacturers, who are eager to point out the difference to you.

A state law requires that mobile homes must have hurricane tie-downs and smoke alarms. The tie-downs are straps that go over the floor and over the roof at intervals, and are attached to anchors buried in the ground for stability. The anchors do double duty as grounding in case lightning strikes. If you put up an antenna, you can attach the grounding wire to one of the stakes.

Be aware of the "standard" and the "optional" features that go with a new mobile home, regardless of what may be in the model home you're shown. Besides being able to upgrade your water heater capacity and electric amperage, there are many other choices you may have. On the exterior you can ask for a larger outside utility shed, a longer driveway, a shingled roof, lap siding instead of sheathing, and a heat pump. Most options are listed on the materials the developer will give you, but some can be custom made for you.

Below are some other features or options you may want to consider. All of them may not be offered for the home you've chosen, but they're suggestions or possibilities to shop through.

covered carport/driveway	roof overhangs
handrails on steps	raised decks
special type of underskirting	screened porch
jalousie windows on porch	hinged doors
concrete slab foundation	sliding glass doors
extra width (26 or 28 feet)	shutter trim
mirror-image orientation	awnings
gutters and downspouts	flower beds
integrated Florida room	copper tubing
bow or bay windows	water softeners

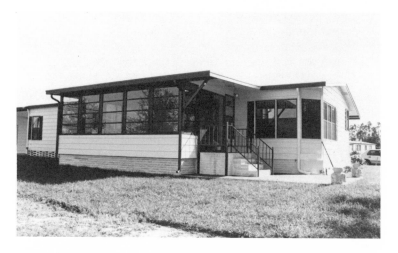

Notice the details of this mobile home: lap siding, enclosed porch, metal railing, downspouts, both solid skirting and loose bricks, newly sodded lawn.

InterCoastal Communities, Inc.

lighted fiberglass steps	separate shower
upgraded insulation	laundry sink
raised ceilings (96″)	double washbowls
extra water cut-off valves	gas for heating, cooking
extra 220-volt line	washer, drier outlets
mercury light switches	relocated ducts
turbine roof ventilators	mirrored closet doors
drywall instead of paneling	wider or longer dimensions.

Besides the above partial list of exterior and construction changes, there may be some of the following you'd like to request for the interior:

garbage disposal	dishwasher
microwave oven	range hood
trash compactor	ice maker
stainless steel sink	water filter
self-cleaning oven	ceramic tiles
upgraded cabinet doors	wet bar
upgraded faucets	built-in desk
washer and drier	door chimes
better carpets and pads	alternate colors

steel shelving in closets	built-in hutch
bookshelves	fireplace
outlets or installed fans	"garden" bathtub
bath vent fans	shower enclosure
Jacuzzi or whirlpool	hand rails
emergency call buttons	ramps
upgraded drapes	extra phone wiring
enameled bathtub	burglar alarm
wall ovens	

Why shouldn't you buy one?

You should know some of the disadvantages. A mobile home is not so substantial as many conventional homes. The walls and cabinets are nearly always made of pressed board faced with plastic. There is little individuality in color schemes. It isn't totally carefree—the outside of the house must be washed twice a year and the heater/air conditioner, filters, and water heaters must be maintained. Unless you buy a home with a shingled roof or one that has had a "roofover," you will have to have the roof coated biennially to keep it from leaking. The appliances, as in any home, develop "bugs," and the pipes for plumbing are polyvinyl chloride, which are more likely to leak than copper.

You have probably read accounts of the vulnerability of mobile homes to high winds. They aren't fastened to a foundation, for one thing, and the roofs aren't attached as securely. Besides those reasons, there are often porches and car ports with metal roofs that overhang and are easily lifted by strong winds.

Less well known, but another serious hazard, is pressed board flooring, which you will find in older homes. If water overflows onto the floors—and many sinks and washbowls and bathtubs don't have overflow drains—you could find your feet literally on the ground. In the mid 80s, regulations were amended to require plywood floors. They're less liable to disintegrate, but they can warp. The bracing under the floor is steel and is adequate for holding pianos, heavy furniture, and crowds of people, but wet flooring can give way.

In the older or less expensive new homes the roof trusses have only a thin metal cover, usually galvanized. The roofing is so light, it's difficult to walk on to do the required coating. Shingles would solve this problem, but unless the trusses are strengthened, they won't support shingles. If you own a home with a sheet metal roof, you can compromise by having a roofover, which consists of sheets of styrofoam covered with a shell of aluminum. This relieves you of the job of coating that a galvanized roof requires, adds a layer of insulation, and doesn't need bracing for support. It should also save you from interior damage by leaks. Depending on the size of the mobile home, a roofover on a doublewide can cost up to $3,000, 1988 prices.

Because of insulating materials and the large amounts of plastic and particleboard used in the construction of a mobile home, formaldehyde fumes may be released into the air. Urea-formaldehyde is considered a potential health hazard, causing breathing problems, skin irritation, and possible cancer. Even healthy persons can have adverse reactions to as little as .01 part per million of the fumes. Ammonia can be used in a process designed to neutralize airborne formaldehyde. Most manufacturers are aware of the problem and are taking steps to minimize or eliminate it. In all fairness, it must be said the problem isn't confined solely to mobile homes. The same products are often used in conventional homes.

Since HUD regulations went into effect in 1976, the incidence of fire is no greater in mobile homes than it is in site-built homes. But when fire does occur in a mobile home, it is more likely to destroy the structure quickly and completely. The plastic materials commonly used are highly combustible and their charring is toxic. All Florida mobile homes are required to have smoke alarms. In addition to the two exits required on mobile homes, most provide windows that allow quick egress from bedrooms. A wise resident mounts extinguishers in strategic locations.

If you want to get some insight into the quality of construction in a mobile home, visit one of the manufacturing plants and see the materials for yourself. You'll find the addresses of the manufacturers in the phone book, and you'll often see their advertisements inviting inspection and offering tours. The trip to the plant will also give you a chance to see their model homes.

Still another way to compare homes so that you can make an intelligent choice is offered at manufactured housing shows presented several times a year at different locations, often on fairgrounds. There you'll see homes made by the many participating plants, and you'll see the many new "luxuries" for the year. The *Florida Statistical Abstract* for 1987 reported 48 builders and 414 dealers in the state handling mobile homes. You can visit them at any time of year.

Finding a good location

If you plan to live in a mobile home park, you may find your choice of homes curtailed. In parks already filled, you will have to buy a used home. The homes hold up well, and you may get quite a bargain. You have a chance to talk to the neighbors already in place about the advantages and disadvantages of life there and of possible difficulties with the owner or the board of directors. You can see how the home looks *in situ* before you buy it; the waiting period before you can move can be very brief; improvements have probably been added by the previous owner; often such homes are sold fully or partially furnished; and—no little benefit—the lawn is already established.

Before you go any further, go to the office to make sure you're eligible to buy, get a copy of the lease and the prospectus to study, and come back later when you have shown them to an attorney.

If you get an OK, next you need to make a careful inspection. If you have any doubts, ask for a termite-free certificate. Check the flow of water in showers, bowls, and toilets. Check the air conditioner to see whether it's running smoothly. Ask about the age of the appliances. Look at the condition of the floorcovering. Inspect the ceilings for stains from possible leaks. Be friendly, but get answers to all your questions. Then go outside and look at the lawn, the siding, the windows and doors, and while you're there, borrow a stepladder to check the roof and gutters.

Take one final step to protect yourself. When you and the owner agree on a price, write out an "agreement of sale" noting the selling price and how it will be paid, the date you will take possession, any contingencies that would let either of you back out of the sale, what furnishings and appliances go with the house, and an acknowledgment that no critical information has been withheld from you. Have it signed and preferably notarized. Then make your down payment. If you change your mind, all you'll lose is that amount.

If you move into a park being developed, you may also have a limited choice among the model homes on display. You might not find the one you fell in love with at the manufacturer's model center. But you'll probably find one reasonably close, and you can always ask whether you can upgrade a model with some of the options suggested.

Very, very few parks will let you bring in your own home, and those that do may have restrictions as to size and orientation. Park owners and operators are in business to make money, and the sale and resale of mobile homes offer a nice return without too much trouble.

The problem of location is greater if you don't want to move into a park. You can have your dream house, but you may not find an ideal place to put it. Don't buy a home or a lot until you first get permission to put the former on the latter. Communities have strict zoning laws which hardly ever allow a mobile home to be set up in the same neighborhood with site-built homes. If you take a drive through some rural or unincorporated areas, you may see mobile homes standing on their own lots. Find a real estate dealer nearby and ask about putting your home there. You may have to have a well dug and a pump and a cesspool installed, and you'll have to deal with the utilities companies yourself, but the local dealer from whom you made your purchase can see to the erection, skirting, and concrete work that your house needs.

What about financial details?

If you apply to a commercial bank for a loan to purchase your home without your own lot, you will probably be offered a simple interest car-type loan. Loans by retirees are usually made only to put cash down on a mobile home while they arrange to sell their old home. In that case a balloon loan for short-term amortization is best. That means the borrower pays only the interest until the period is up, at which time the principal is due.

If retirees want to make long-term payments similar to those on a home, they can apply to a savings and loan, which offers 15-year monthly payments for new homes in a qualifying park. The bank's name is on the title as lien holder until the debt is paid.

Loans for older homes have shorter maturity dates depending on the age of the home. A down payment of 20% is the most common in loans for both old and new homes. Managers of developments have contacts and can recommend a bank, if you wish. Truth-in-lending laws apply.

In a typical transaction for a cash sale you will put a third down when you choose the lot and home, a third on delivery, and the final third when the home is erected and you take possession. These percentages vary from development to development, but in all cases the final payment is due when you move in.

If you want to reserve a space for a home to be chosen later, you have to make a minimum financial commitment or pay a year's ground rent in advance. Should you choose your home, too, at the time you reserve a lot, you should ask to have the price frozen and the deal put in writing, but you'll have to make the usual deposit on the home. In some parks where the owners are anxious to attract buyers, you may be able to persuade the salesman to apply the advance rent money to the purchase of the home if you keep your part of the deal.

Don't be too anxious to settle on the price you're quoted. Ask questions. Make an offer of your own. If that isn't successful, see whether you can get an option or free rent for a certain period. You might have walked into a buyer's market. Also, see whether you can talk yourself into an advantage on the terms of the contract you'll have to sign. There's important information about that contract in the next chapter.

Will your home depreciate in value? That depends on many factors: the location, the prices of conventional homes, the care and maintenance given, and the conditions in the rental park. Insurance rates show an overall slow appreciation, but that's not always reflected in resale prices.

Taking care of the new home

In some ways there is low maintenance on the home. You don't have to paint the exterior if it's aluminum siding, and even the galvanized vertical siding doesn't need a new coat for years. Pipes aren't going to burst from freezing, nor will concrete crack from cold. Appliances are new, along with carpet and drapes. New-home warranty takes care of any problems that arise at least for the first year.

Complaints to the manufacturer are usually handled promptly and corrections made. The problems with a new home may range from discarded scraps of building materials pushing up lumps in the carpet to sewage pipes that some workman neglected to connect with the mains. There are divided responsibilities for different shortcomings: the dealer, the manufacturer, the setup men, and the park management. One or the other should come to your rescue, but in case you aren't satisfied, write to the Department of Highway Safety and Motor Vehicles, Division of Motor Vehicles, Bureau of Mobile Home and Recreational Vehicle Construction, Tallahassee, Fl 32301.

By the time your warranty is up, all the required corrections and adjustments should have been made. The one major problem that outlives the warranty is the settling of the house. If it's not on stable ground, it could develop a lean. That's serious because of what happens to the framework and the utility connections. A workman can level the home by jacking it up and adding the necessary shims to the supports. That won't increase the stability of the soil, however, and you might like to check periodically with a level to see whether it needs to be done again.

The roof, as noted before, needs attention if it isn't shingled or treated with a roofover. Within six to twelve months after you move in, it should be coated for the first time. A year later another coat is required to keep it waterproof and rustproof. Thereafter every two years should be enough. You can hire a workman to do the job or do it yourself. The material can be bought from an aluminum or building materials place for $55 a five-gallon drum (1988 prices). The first coating for a double-wide would most likely require two drums, and subsequent coatings should take about half that much. It's a hot job to put it on with the sun reflecting off the white roof, and you must be careful to walk on the supported areas while you work.

Check the tie-downs occasionally. Some parts are subject to rust. The metal screws in the siding and trim on your house are not likely to be made of stainless steel, and eventually these will rust and the discoloration will run down the exterior. The best way to deal with this if you don't want to replace the screws with the expensive stainless kind is to coat the galvanized screws before they can rust. You may also be able to find the little plastic caps that can be pressed on to protect the screw heads. (On lap siding there are few exposed screws.) If you have ordered awnings installed, make sure the supports have been fastened to something more substantial than the siding, and check those screws for rust, too.

The lawn is another headache. The coarse grass may look like something you would have pulled out in a Northern lawn. To be kept nice it requires fertilization several times a year. The sandy soil doesn't hold nutrients long. Also, the hot sun and the generous rainfall keep it growing at a great rate in the summertime. If you're not in a development where the mowing is done for you, you've got a steady job. Even if a maintenance crew mows your lawn, they aren't likely to rake the clippings or trim the edges. And if the grass grows, so do the weeds.

One answer that more and more thoughtful people are using is to "go natural" and employ ground covers and shrubs that not only give you freedom from lawn care and the use of fertilizers and poisons, but also give you a more esthetic diversity to look out on. You'll attract more birds, and your life will be enriched as well as eased.

You can also treat the house pests by environmentally safe methods. One inexpensive and effective remedy to keep roaches out of your kitchen drawers and shelves is to place a single boric acid pellet in each one. Explain what they are so no one around you thinks they're ordinary pills, and especially warn any young children that visit you. Birds and spiders and praying mantises are good controls for bugs and grubs. Hot water takes care of ant hills, and traps catch many garden pests.

Let's have a little positive thinking. You're not going to have to shovel snow. Nobody is likely to track mud into your house. The windowsills of most Florida homes aren't yet polluted by industrial dust. The plastic walls, although they have a sameness and artificiality that you may deplore, stay clean for a long time, and then respond to a bit of soap and water. And when you're retired, there are only adults in the house most of the time. Your furniture will last a long while, and your appliances and rugs hardly ever need replacement.

Setting up the mobile home

Every time you drive along a numbered highway in Florida you can take odds that you'll see at least one truck bearing the caution "Wide Load" and hauling a mobile home or section. Somewhere that truck is going to turn into the two-lane streets of a mobile home park, and inside the park to back up into a narrow lot between two other mobile homes. If the driver has carried half a doublewide, his co-worker will arrive shortly with the other half and neatly put it on the lot next to the part already there. The final juggling is done by a tractor, which gives a judicious nudge here and there on the least vulnerable portions of the future home.

Then workers swarm over the jointed areas of the home, sealing, fastening, and integrating them with overlapping parts. Inside, the ceilings and floors are matched and the joints concealed with a "marriage board." The carpet and padding are lined up so that the seams are nearly invisible.

The new home is mounted on concrete and cinderblock pillars on footers at 10-foot intervals. The hitch, the axles, and the wheels are removed and returned to the factory for recycling.

Along the sides of the home the tie-down straps are attached to the anchor rods, which are driven into the ground. Hookups must be made to water, sewer, electric, telephone, and cable lines. Steps, usually of precast concrete, are set in place before the doors.

If you're there to watch this miracle, you can go in shortly and check it out. Are the cupboard doors split? Are screws in straight? Is the floor level? Is there debris under the carpet? Do the electrical outlets all operate and is the load distributed fairly among the circuits? Were plugs provided in the wash basins? Does hot water come out of the right spigot? Is the sewer connection made? Does the roof leak? Does heat or air conditioning come through all the outlets? Do all appliances and accessories work? Do windows and doors open smoothly? Is there an unacceptable gap between the bottoms of the interior doors and the floor? Do the keys fit? Do traverse rods operate? Is the electric panelboard marked to identify the circuits? Do the drawers slide out readily and the cupboard doors operate as they should? Are the towel bars straight? Is the main water turnoff valve accessible, and do the individual ones throughout the house all work? Have all the options you chose been included?

Don't move in yet, though. Your home isn't finished until it has at least a driveway and underskirting. Nearly always there will be an aluminum roof over the driveway and a small utility shed, which will not only add to your comfort, but also make the place look bigger and more homelike. Part of the package with the purchase of your house is the installation of the driveway, skirting, finished car port, gutters, downspouts, and steps.

The underskirting needs to be removable for several reasons. First, you don't want a solid wall. It can get hot or damp or moldy under the floors if you seal out the flow of air. Second, pipes and cables and wiring crisscross underneath. Sooner or later you will need access to them all. Most buyers prefer unmortared bricks laid in an alternating pattern with air spaces between each brick, but plastic or aluminum strips that can be screwed to supports are an alternate choice. You may have to conform to the pattern adopted by the park.

Sometimes homeowners use this under-the-house space for storing bulky items like ladders. Objections are the possible deterioration of the stored items, their interference with utility connections, the danger of flooding, and damage from any infestation of rodents or insects.

The front of the house usually has a skirting of mortared bricks or of cinderblock faced with stone for the sake of appearance. You can use it as a backdrop for a raised flower bed to "anchor" your house to the landscape. Think well before you yield to the temptation to add more beds or to plant a tree if you have a short offset from the street. It will interfere with mowing and crowd your space. Big trees are great for natural temperature control if you have plenty of room for them, but most mobile home lots are skimpy. You're lucky if you find a park where the developer has preserved the trees.

Before you put up a hi-fi or CB antenna, check with the management of the park and the local code. You'll need good support from the ground because the roof will not bear the weight. The height of the antenna must fit the park rules, and the state law says for safety's sake antennas must be grounded eight feet deep. You can probably simply connect to a tie-down.

Paying the tax collector

If your home is on rented ground, you don't have to pay property taxes—directly. You can just be sure they're included in your rent. Since the landlord doesn't get a household exemption for his business, your taxes would be higher than those of a landowner except that your lot isn't likely to be as big as his. The taxes are probably equivalent when all is toted up. But they don't stop there. You can end up paying more than the person with the real property.

It came about because tradition is hard to kill. When mobile homes were considered trailers to drag around behind your car or truck, they had to have license tags. The same tags are required by the Bureau of Motor Vehicles, but they no longer come in metal plates that you must mount on your home. They've metamorphosed into decals. Every January you go to your county motor vehicle office to buy your decal, which you stick in the lower corner of the window nearest the street on which your home rests. If you have a doublewide, you have to get *two* decals. For a 60-ft. single in 1988 the fee was $50. Beginning at a base of $20, the cost rises in increments of $5 for each increase of five feet in length. That's the second tax on renters.

The third is a tangible tax levied on every structure not integral to the house: the covered carport, the utility building, the screened porch, and the garage, if any. This varies depending on the community and the extras you've added, but you're looking at an average of $40-50.

Then there's the fourth. The person who put his mobile home on a single lot paid this, too, but the owner of a conventional home didn't. Just as though you were buying a car, you have to pay the state sales tax on your mobile home. In 1988 this was 6% or 7%, depending on which county you live in. That adds $3,000 or $3,500 to the price of a $50,000 home.

Other charges

While you're planning for the expenses of your new home, don't forget the one-time charges for hooking up utilities and for installing phone jacks. Expect to need little things that send you to the housewares and hardware stores and to plant nurseries. Take care of your transfers of title and notifications of address change.

But the biggest extra expense is likely to be homeowners' insurance. It's high on mobile homes. The cost in 1988 of a policy with the following coverage with a $250 deductible was between $325 and $350 a year:

> $50,000 on the dwelling
> 50,000 on the contents
> 15,000 for loss of use
> 50,000 personal liability
> 1,000 medical coverage for guests

A mobile home that is flooded is virtually worthless. You pay a high premium for your home insurance, so be sure you're covered for flooding. You still may lose many personal things perhaps more valuable to you than the things that insurance will replace. If you have to collect on a flooding claim due to an "act of God" and not to some overflow in the home, ask yourself whether you want a home rebuilt on the same site with the same vulnerability.

It takes time to follow all the recommendations above, but you now have knowledge to help you make intelligent choices, and you can feel more confident about your future. You can be very happy in your mobile home if you choose the right park. Please read Chapter 6 to find out what it's like to live in a mobile home park, what your legal rights are, and how to protect them.

6. Living in a Rental Park

Mobile homes usually end up in a park because an old prejudice against them keeps them from being zoned side-by-side with conventional homes in most communities. With restrictions, they are allowed in outlying areas, but not in towns—unless they're clustered together in their own enclave called a park, a reminder of the fact that they're classified as vehicles.

There are two kinds of parks: those in which you rent the ground on which your home is placed, and those in which you "own" your lot. In the latter case you don't really own it in the sense that you have a title in fee simple; you own a share in the park, and that means in common terms, you have joined a condominium. You pay your share of taxes directly after the homestead exemption. You pay no ground rent, but you pay your share of upkeep on the common facilities, the roads, the administrative expenses, and any costs resulting from a lawsuit.

This chapter is about the rental park, and the next one will concern itself with condominiums, whether for apartments, "villas," "patio homes," or mobile homes.

Although there are a growing number of resident-owned parks, in the large majority of mobile home parks the tenants pay

rent for the ground on which their homes stand and their entitlement to certain amenities and common areas.

Rental communities have several advantages. The first is the
control exercised by a professional management that can make
and enforce rules. The centralized control can keep the park well
maintained and can receive complaints, keep records, sell
homes, and oversee day-to-day operations. Second, through not
having to purchase a lot, the renter can keep from tying up more
of his money and can probably resell his home more readily.
Third, the stated rent often includes municipal services, such as
water and sewer and sanitation, which relieves the homeowner
from paying separate bills.

Of course, by its very nature, putting a valuable home on land
that someone else owns is a risky business. As pointed out in
the preceding chapter, it's costly to remove an already erected
mobile home. A tenant is more or less a captive of the park
owner if there is no redress for what he considers arbitrary rules
or unjustified rent increases. You need to take a look at the ways
to protect yourself that are discussed in this chapter.

In the meantime, let's see what it's like to live in a park.

The neighbors

Most mobile home parks are for retirees, but many take working families as well. It's advisable for retirees to move into an
"adult only" park, where the restrictions on age may begin at
any figure above 18, but usually specify 40 or more. In practice
this means that most of the residents are retired, but a few
empty-nesters or childless couples are still in the work force.
The age restrictions have been judged legal by the 5th District
Court of Appeal in Daytona Beach in the case of a subdivision,
and in 1979 the Florida Supreme Court upheld the validity of
age restrictions in a condominium where the association prohibited children younger than 12.

There is a tendency for the population of parks to attract people with common backgrounds or places of origin. The special
interests represented may be groups such as retired teachers,

people with the same religious beliefs, or those from the same state. This is especially true of parks small enough for the residents to know each other. There are no mobile home parks where the population is wholly black or where blacks form a majority. A few larger parks have some black residents, but they're the exception. More than 99% of the residents of recognized mobile home parks are white. Of course, no one can be discriminated against because of his race nor for any reason that violates his civil rights. It's custom, and not law, that's responsible for this phenomenon.

A demographic survey of mobile home residents conducted by Florida State University College of Business and funded by the state revealed the following profile of mobile home residents:

(1) 88.3% were originally from another state. In order the five top states were Michigan, New York, Ohio, Illinois, and Pennsylvania.
(2) 75.8% were married couples
(3) Average number of persons per home: 1.83
(4) Average age of residents: 70.2 years
(5) 91% were fully retired; 5.5% were semi-retired.

Characteristics of a park

Parks usually provide a clubhouse, paved and lighted streets, a laundry and drying yard, shrubbery in the common areas, sodding throughout, and underground utility connections. Often there are a swimming pool and courts for outdoor games. There may be other amenities as well, including 18-hole golf courses. Postal boxes in a rental park are usually located in a spot near the clubhouse or in neighborhood clusters in larger parks.

Most mobile home lots are small, for the benefit of the developer, who can get more return that way, and for the homeowner, who has less ground to take care of. A typical lot in older parks may be 80 by 45 feet, allowing for 10 feet between homes, but zoning laws in municipalities now tend to demand more separation between houses. The larger and more deluxe parks space the homes farther apart and include more trees and landscaping.

An attractive clubhouse facing a waterfront in a Ft. Lauderdale park.

InterCoastal Communities, Inc.

If you have a choice of lot, you may want to choose one with an east-west axis and the major rooms facing south. This orientation is recommended by architects as best for comfort, energy saving, and light distribution in Florida. Admittedly, it's hard to achieve in a mobile home park, for they're usually placed narrow-side front in rows. You may have to compromise on "morning sun in the kitchen" or whatever pleases you and achieve what comfort you can with trees, awnings, or a wide overhang.

There are a few things you can control even if you can't achieve the ideal orientation of your home. It might not be a good idea to choose a lot on the outside edge of a park where the neighboring lots are empty and may be developed in a manner you don't like. For coolness, have the carport as a buffer on the western (hottest) side of your house. Be sure, too, that an entrance is on the same side as the carport, or it will be most inconvenient. And last, look at the length of the driveway. Even after you have built a screened porch and accommodated the utility shed under the carport roof, you'll need room for your car and at least one guests' car.

Locating a park

Mobile home parks are clustered in areas of the state in the configuration of a gigantic letter H. The two verticals are the east and west coasts and the broad horizontal bands join them across Central Florida from Ocala on the north to Lake Okeechobee on the south. These areas are more likely to be congested, metropolitan, expensive, and convenient to urban amenities. Northern Florida and the Panhandle are less heavily populated, more rural, cooler by a few degrees, and somewhat cheaper.

When you've chosen the region you prefer, visit parks in the area to see which ones you like. Consider some of these factors:

How many units are in the park?

Which roads give access to it, and how congested are they?

Are there city fire and police protection?

Are adequate medical facilities nearby?

Is it within reasonable distance of shopping, churches, banks, restaurants, and entertainment?

What is the source and quality of the water supply?

Is mass transit available?

How close is the airport?

Are there cultural opportunities: libraries, museums, theaters, musical groups, universities, and state parks or other natural preserves?

What recreational facilities are close by: fishing, race tracks, beaches, boating, golf, bowling, and sports stadiums, for example?

Is the area vulnerable to high winds and flooding?

How is drainage in the streets?

What's on the television cable?

Is there a limit on the pickup of trash?

Is the swimming pool large enough? Is it clean?

Are the clubhouse facilities adequate for the park population?

How are after-hours emergencies handled?

Is there access to water, including a boat ramp and marina?

With more than 6,000 mobile home parks in Florida, a prospective buyer has a wide choice. In some cases it's a buyers' market. A hard-to-fill park or a new one getting off the ground sometimes offers free or low-cost visitation programs in which you live in the community or in a nearby motel for a few days while you talk to tenants and join in the activities of the park. To separate the lookers from the serious prospective buyers, the parks offering visitations often safeguard themselves by making the visitor pay a small part of the costs himself. Needless to say, this is an excellent way to preview a park. If the park in which you're interested doesn't offer a visitation program, do it yourself.

The number of units in a park has significance. A development with 100 to 300 homes is one where you will get to know almost all your neighbors. This could be important, for retirees tend to be concerned about each other, and in sicknesses or emergencies they're very helpful. In a park with fewer, say 25 to 99 homes, again the people are friendly, but there are hardly enough persons to hold group activities. When the number of residences rises to a thousand or more, you have a self-contained, unincorporated "town," and the offering of activities and services has increased geometrically. In such a park your voice in affairs is often lost. The tendency is for expansion of existing parks and for larger and larger concentrations where desirable land is still available. It's a big business today.

You might want a checklist of offerings to find those that are important to you before you make your decision.

heated swimming pool	cable TV
waterfront lots	lawn mowing
outdoor barbecue	picnic area
volleyball courts	bike trails
golf course	shuttle bus
softball field	sauna or spa
shuffleboard courts	putting green
boccie, horseshoes	tennis courts

ping-pong tables	marina
RV parking	security force
emergency medics	jogging trails
laundry and yard	workshop

There is a critical question to ask before you choose *any* park or decide to build in an undeveloped area. Both may look fine covered with vegetation and adjacent to a beautiful lake or an estuary leading to the ocean. But whether the site is an ecologically sound place for homes to be built, whether it will be subject to flood and hurricane damage, whether it will be viable economically, are only a few of the questions that an uninformed person is unable to answer. Asking residents how safe the environment is may not give you a sufficient answer, for the forces of nature behave erratically, and just because an area has not been flooded recently doesn't mean that it might not happen. You'll find more information about this in the chapter entitled "The Endangered Environment." You could pay your insurance and take your chance with the rest of the residents, or if you're bothered with the prospect, you can check with the city hall or the water management district to see whether the land lies on a floodplain.

Activities

A park with a sufficiently large number of residents is sure to have some group activities. These range in scope from those organized by a paid recreational director to those begun and operated by the residents. You're not required to participate at all, but you may well find others with similar interests that you can enjoy together. Here's yet another list to guide you in inquiring about activities.

arts and crafts	bingo
residents' association	card games
coffee hours	newsletter
social dancing	library
bands and combos	choruses
blood pressure checks	bicycling
square dancing	table tennis
potluck dinners	shuffleboard

The good life in a mobile home park can include such amenities as the chickee hut "gazebo" and the beautifully tiled spa shown in this picture.

InterCoastal Communities, Inc.

pancake breakfasts	fishing
athletic teams	hobbies
aerobic dancing	ceramics
organized travel	gardening
sewing classes	field trips
bazaars and rummage sales	billiards
weight control	exercise
men's, women's clubs	Bible study
Spanish classes	chess
photo darkroom	boat rental
in-park movies	drama groups

Signing the contract

You've had to compromise. As in the rest of this life, you haven't gotten everything you wish. But you've made up your mind. This is the right region, the right park, and the right home. Now for the legal ramifications.

The operation of mobile home parks is governed by Florida Statutes 723 and administered by the Department of Business Regulation, Division of Land Sales, Condominiums, and

Mobile Homes, 725 South Bronough Street, Tallahassee, Fl 32301.

Before you move in, the manager or salesman must present you with a prospectus. This is a document described in great detail in the statutes, and will provide you with full disclosure of these principal items: name of the park owner and legal address, description of the park, recreational and other common facilities for your use, hours when these are available, any improvements that are contemplated, which services are included in your rent, how rents may be raised, any "pass-through" and all other charges you may have to pay, the current rules and regulations of the park, the existing zoning, a map, and a copy of the rental agreement offered to you.

Don't try to read this on the spot. Take it with you and study it. Before you sign the prospectus or the lease, you'll want to have a lawyer read them. Don't think it's safe for you to take a chance just because all the residents in the park have signed such a paper. Be sure *yourself* what it means.

While the prospectus is your guarantee of certain rights, the lease agreement is the document that contains your obligations. The typical lease sets the payment of your starting rent and the term of rental, usually a year. It will specify that the term is renewable, for the safeguards of the law provide that you can't be evicted without cause. What is important to you is the next piece of information: what limitation is there on the rent increases?

The tendency in regard to leases in parks today is to tie the rent increases to the Consumer Price Index. This is a figure calculated by the Office of Prices and Living Conditions in the Bureau of Labor Statistics of the U.S. Department of Labor. The office considers seven categories in arriving at the index: housing, which includes fuel and furnishings; apparel and its upkeep; transportation; medical care; entertainment; and other goods and services.

It affects all American consumers in many ways, controlling increases in government benefits, including social security. It's measured by comparing current prices with those of the previous year to see whether or how much they have increased. The CPI used in the figures below shows the social security increase for the year given based on the rise the previous year.

1980	14.3%
1981	11.2
1982	7.4
1983	0
1984	3.5
1985	3.5
1986	3.1
1987	1.3
1988	4.2

For your purposes, this is as fair a deal as you can get provided the starting rent is reasonable. It isn't an exact measure of the services you receive, for as you see above, it's based on some factors that don't apply to rent, but it's at least a tool furnished by a disinterested party. Read the CPI cap paragraphs carefully, nevertheless, for many contain the provision that the rent will not be *reduced* if the CPI goes down and others say the increase will be the CPI or another stated percentage, whichever is higher.

You have a right to be concerned by "pass-through" charges, as described in the prospectus, which is considered part of your lease. The amounts are not specified, but whatever these charges are, you will be billed for your pro-rata share. They're restricted by law to government-imposed charges, such as increases in water rates and in property taxes or a ruling requiring the installation of a new sewer system. Just tell yourself you'd have to pay them in a conventional home or by increased rent in an apartment.

The terms of the lease expire when you sell the home or try to pass it on to your heirs. It's common for the lease you held to continue in force until the next expiration date. After that the new owner must sign a lease on whatever terms he is offered and agrees to.

Legal protections for the landlord are written last in the lease: you must pay the rent or be evicted (one of the causes permitted by law), you must follow the rules which he sets, you must pay his legal fees to collect delinquencies, you must vacate the premises in case of a change in land use. You can, however, occupy his land and use the common facilities.

The landlord/tenant relations are governed by Florida Statutes 723, as stated above. Get a copy by writing to the address given, for they're your safeguard. They're written in reasonably simple English and administered by the Department of Business Regulation. You almost certainly won't be alone in assuring the protection of your rights, for any friction between the landlord and the tenants eventually leads to the formation of a homeowners association.

The homeowners association is an incorporated entity that officially represents the tenants in any dispute with the park owners. And these disputes arise frequently from true or perceived injustices. Associations are impowered to seek redress by submitting complaints of violations or statements of dispute to the DBR. The Department may fine a park owner or the association for violations of the law, but it can't adjudicate disputed matters. The final authority in the settlement of disputes is to be found in suits brought before courts of law.

Chapter 723 of the Statutes, which superseded previous chapters regarding mobile homes, was first signed into law on June 1, 1984. In subsequent years amendments were made and no doubt will continue to be made in years to come. Among the provisions are these obligations of the landlord: to pay certain fees for the administration of the law; to disclose full information in a prospectus to be given to each lessee; to engage in no false advertising; to demonstrate good faith and fair dealing; to promulgate reasonable rules and regulations; to resettle tenants or reimburse them for the costs of their homes if he sells the land for some other use; not to harass associations nor restrict their right to operate; not to charge "unconscionable" rent nor reduce his services without reducing the rent proportionately; not to evict tenants without legally specified cause; and finally, to offer the park to the tenants for the right of first refusal in case he has found a buyer.

Affecting homeowners associations are the following: incorporation as the representative of the park tenants; abiding by specified rules for the structure of the organization; compliance with prescribed (and often complicated) procedures for complaints, disputes, negotiations, mediation, and arbitration; qualifying to act as agents for possible purchase of the park.

The grounds for eviction are limited to nonpayment of rent; conviction of violation of a law or ordinance that is detrimental to health, safety, and welfare of the residents; second violation of a proper rule or regulation; failure to qualify as a tenant.

The description above of the terms of the Chapter is a very general summary, and is not a legal interpretation of the meaning and intent of the law. All tenants are encouraged to ask for a copy from the source and read it for themselves. Fortunately, it provides you with a final escape mechanism. You have a grace period of 15 days to change your mind even after you have signed a lease.

Park rules and regulations

A copy of the rules of the park is supplied in the prospectus. For the most part they aren't onerous to obey and they protect the neighborhood. They're common today in subdivisions of homes and in condominiums as well as in mobile home parks. Nevertheless, prospective buyers are advised to read them over and determine whether they're a set of rules they wish to live by. Common provisions are these:

>description of how the rules can be changed
>restrictions on age and number of residents per unit
>restrictions on the stay of guests
>control of visiting children
>responsibilities for use of common facilities
>description of permitted appurtenances to the house
>restrictions on antennas and clotheslines
>care of grass and shrubbery

prohibition or control of pets
proper refuse disposal
prohibition of car repairs on premises
considerate and quiet occupation
disclaimer of management's responsibility for
    damages.

Extra living costs

After you have accepted the offered rent rate, which will probably fall between $100 and $300 a month, you will have to pay the annual taxes and insurance and the utility bills. Of course, the municipal services of water, sewer, and trash collection are often included in the stated rent. If not, you can use the estimated amounts below as a rough guide. These monthly figures are average for Central Florida for a 1400-square-foot doublewide home in a mid-sized park:

lot rental, including sanitation	$150
water and sewer services	35
cable TV (group rate)	10
taxes on tangible property	4
license tags	8
homeowners' insurance	27
electricity	75
telephone	25
total	$334

If you rent a boat slip or space for keeping your recreational vehicle, those will probably be additional.

Owner/tenant relations

Calling the resident of a mobile home park a "tenant" is a misnomer. He's really a homeowner, and his rights have to be weighed in the balance with those of the landowner. The suggestion was made above that in effect the homeowner is at the mercy of the park owner, and that this has caused grief in many instances.

Most sizable parks today are owned by limited partnerships or corporations that are looking for the best return for the money they can earn for their shareholders. There is no personal give and take between the owners and the renters, and often legitimate grievances arise. There have been bitter court fights, lengthy and expensive, usually followed by equally long and expensive appeals. Sometimes these concern rules made by the owners and sometimes alleged harassment or illegal evictions.

But the most common complaint of the homeowners is the escalating rent and the thorny question of what constitutes unconscionability. Since the laws have been on the books for only a few years, there is no appreciable body of case law to guide a judge in deciding a suit, and the lack of precedent has clouded the issues. In the 1988 session the legislature set up a committee to look into the question of unconscionability.

There is no question that rents in many parks have risen all out of proportion to the rest of the economy. In many cases this was because of the rapid turnover of park owners. Investors offer to buy a park at a much higher price than its just valuation by the county tax office and a lot more than the former owner paid for it, for the word has gotten around that parks are a profitable venture with an all but guaranteed return. Then to compensate for the inflated investment, they raise the rents. In a few years the scenario repeats itself and the rents continue the upward spiral of escalation.

On the side of the homeowners is the 25-year-old Federation of Mobile Home Owners of Florida, Inc., whose address is P.O. Box 5350, Largo, Fl 34649. The FMO is funded by a substantial and growing number of individual owners and has established units in hundreds of mobile home parks. It has a legal staff, publishes a newsletter and bulletins, has a record of many successes, and is the principal voice lobbying on behalf of the mobile home owners in the state legislature. Dues are low, in the neighborhood of $10 a year per home. A wise homeowner will benefit by joining the organization.

The sheer numbers of persons living in mobile home parks bring significant pressure on the state government to affect changes. Statutes 723 was such an accomplishment, and while it hasn't been perfect, it has been revised and fine-tuned every year since it was first passed. Until its protection is complete, the mobile home buyer must insist on at least a stated limit in his lease on the amount of increase in rent allowed in a year.

Beware of oral promises. Whatever isn't written and signed, may be as ephemeral as the words. Your lease, when you have decided to accept it, is valid as of that date, and the terms can't be changed. If the lease and the prospectus, which is part of it, don't list a charge, you don't have to pay it. If the park is subsequently sold to someone else, he inherits your lease. The courts have affirmed this. Don't sign a new one unless it's better than the one you already have.

The permanence of a lease is a great advantage if you can get special concessions like a lifetime guaranteed rent. They're hard to find today, for this is no longer the era of the unsophisticated single owner, but sometimes inducements are made in parks that are filling slowly.

Selling or subletting your home

If you're dissatisfied with your move or if circumstances require you to locate elsewhere, you can offer it for sale. The law says you have the right to sell it yourself. Your "for sale" sign may have to conform to park rules, but you are allowed to put it up. You may advertise it in newspapers. You may hold an open house unless there are security problems. You may put it in the hands of a real estate salesman for his usual fee, but not all dealers are qualified to sell a mobile home, which is considered a chattel and not a piece of real estate. You may also have the management sell it for you, but you'll have to pay the commission for their services. In 1988 this averaged 7%.

When you have a qualified buyer who isn't ready to move in at once, get him to sign an agreement of sale. It should identify the buyer, seller, property to be transferred, amount of money involved, amount of down payment, terms and dates by which the transaction will be completed, what if anything can nullify it, and a stipulation of the items, such as furnishings, to be included in the sale.

If a qualified buyer wants to close at once, get your title and go with him to the county tag office where the clerks will collect the sales tax and transfer the title to the new owner.

You can also sublet your home within the restrictions of the park rules. The renters must be in the acceptable age group and you must inform the office of their presence. You and the tenants agree among yourselves on the amount and term of the rental. Unless the prospectus allows management to charge a fee for locating the renter, overseeing the place, or performing services in your absence, it cannot collect any share of the rent you receive. How much is that? It depends on many variables, but it will probably be within the range of $400 to $1,000 a month, not including electricity. Part of the proceeds will be spent on an insurance rider to cover renting your property, and part for any lawn care you contract for.

If you make your Florida mobile home your winter residence and live in your home state the rest of the year, you will probably find the home is safe in your absence, but there are a few precautions to observe. Arrange for your mail to be forwarded and give your key to the manager or a reliable neighbor to check on the house now and then. When you notify the phone company, ask about special rates that apply to absences of a certain number of months. You can have the gas turned off, too, but you must keep the electricity. You need the latter to keep the air conditioner going and any maintenance lights. Set the air conditioner at about 88 degrees to keep down humidity and mold.

Drain the hotwater heater; turn off the water; open the closet doors; notify the newspaper delivery man. Put down charcoal for humidity and bug pellets for pests. Give your summer address to concerned persons, including the police and the insurance company.

Take your irreplaceables and valuables with you, and there shouldn't be much left to attract thieves. In many parks two-thirds of the residents leave for the summer. Have fun and forget your Florida home. Chances are excellent for your finding everything in place and ready to go when the frost chases you back.

In case vandalism or other acts of malicious mischief occur after your dwelling has been vacant for more than 30 consecutive days, it is most likely that your standard homeowners' policy won't cover the loss. Ask. The chance isn't great in a park where the homes are close together. Go ahead and take it. Nothing is certain in this life.

Enough about mobile homes. It's time to turn our attention to other kinds of housing. Let's investigate some alternatives: apartments, single homes, cooperatives, condominiums, and retirement care facilities.

7. Condominiums and Cooperatives

The Department of Housing and Human Services reported that on January 1, 1986, half the condominiums in the United States were in Florida. There were almost 21,000 of them with well over a million units and 2.5 million residents. They aren't all physically alike. The range is from deluxe highrises of 40 stories to an enclave of a few dozen townhouses or cluster homes or a resident-owned mobile home park. But because the unit owners share certain costs in common, they all fall within the definition of a condominium.

The first statewide law to regulate them began in 1975, and is in effect today as Florida Statutes 718, popularly known as the "Condominium Act." If you choose a condominium for your retirement home, ask for a copy from the Department of Business Regulation, Division of Florida Land Sales, Condominiums and Mobile Homes, 725 S. Bronough St., Tallahassee, Fl 32301. There are two branch offices: 1313 N. Tampa Street, Tampa 33606, and 1350 N.W. 12th Avenue, Miami 33125.

Is buying a condo a good idea? Considering how many people live in them, it would seem so, but is that all a buyer should consider? Let's look further and see what's attractive and what isn't so good.

Condominium or cooperative?

Both condominiums and cooperatives are homes in which the residents share some kind of joint ownership, but the differences between them are important.

In an apartment-type condo a purchaser buys the interior of his unit and pays a monthly fee for the upkeep of his share in the common facilities, such as swimming pool, lobby, tennis courts, parking lot, shrubbery, water pipes, and the exterior parts of the building, among others. He has paid for his unit, and the state will allow him a homestead exemption on it if it's his primary domicile. In a co-op he buys a share of stock in the corporation that owns the building and is considered a "proprietary tenant," or tenant/owner, who shares the expenses of operation and enjoys the amenities provided.

Both of these are specific legal concepts of owning land and living space. Both are governed by a contract, its bylaws, rules and regulations, and boards of directors elected by the residents. Both have to contribute to the maintenance of the facilities.

The condo owner's fees are set as a percentage of the total upkeep based on the size and location of his unit. The co-op resident has an equal voice with the other members of his group regardless of the number of shares he may hold. The co-op owner is more financially vulnerable, for if the other shareholders default, he must pay their share. As an example of the differences in practice, consider what happens if there is a foreclosure. The condo owner still retains his equity, but the co-op owner stands to lose his total investment.

Condos are much more common today although cooperatives still exist in which the members have lived peaceably together without having disaster strike.

Kinds of condos

Condominiums come in many forms: a tenant-owned mobile home park, a group of townhouses set in an enclave with private streets and a clubhouse with perhaps some recreational facilities, a converted apartment house, a highrise, in some cases a single home in a development, or something in between. The main characteristic is owning some features in common with others, for condominium derives from Latin words meaning joint rule.

When you buy a condo in a multi-unit structure, you are buying the space between the floor and ceiling and the walls of your unit. You own shares in the electric wiring and plumbing pipes, the roof of the building, the walls and foundations, the elevators, the recreational facilities, and the entrance area. You have to pay a fee for their maintenance and repair or replacement. The common property of the condominium unit owners is governed by a board of directors elected by the members according to the percentage equivalent of each unit, determined usually by its size

Condominiums and apartment buildings line a
beach at Marco Island.

or location. Fees are charged for use of the facilities whether a member uses them or not.

There are advantages to living in a condo. For one thing, you have such things as swimming pools and tennis courts that you might not be able to own yourself. You don't have to mow the lawn, trim the bushes, nor paint the outside of the building. There is often someone to screen visitors, providing you with a degree of security. You may be able to live in a "better" neighborhood, and you may be saving money by building equity or by deducting financing charges and claiming the homestead exemption.

The disadvantages are sharing power with others with whom you may not agree, and facing repair charges for some things that don't immediately benefit you. The same problems that face residents in mobile home parks—increased charges and decrease in services—can occur in condos. You will have to find a buyer if you want to move, and resale condo units may be harder to sell. If major repairs are made, you must pay your share in the form of assessments. The other disadvantage is common to other shared living facilities: difficulties with the neighbors.

Buying a condo

If you're considering buying a condo unit, first look at a number of them to get a feeling for what is available and what you can afford. You don't, of course, have to pay the asking price, especially on a second-hand unit. You might want to hire an appraiser to learn what the unit is truly worth and what flaws he can find in the property.

For a rough way to judge whether the price is right, you can do a bit of arithmetic. By looking in the newspaper ads, by applying at apartment houses, or by checking with real estate agents who handle apartments, you can determine the going rent for an apartment with the number of square feet you will have in the condo you've chosen. Let's say you come up with $500.

Now take the amount asked for the condo, say $50,000, and figure how much it would earn in a safe investment, such as a

A section of small, two-level homes commonly found in apartment or condominium complexes.

Matsche Real Estate Company

certificate of deposit or a savings bond, say 8%. This would return $334 a month in interest to reduce the apartment rent. Add to the rent the amount of federal income tax you would have to pay on the $4,000 you received as interest on the tax (in the 28% bracket annually $1,120, monthly $93). The homestead exemption would apply to half the local taxes on the home, $33 a month, which must be added to the condo account.

Apartment rent	$500
Interest on $50,000	− 334
IRS tax on 50,000	+ 93
Total monthly cost	$259
Condo fees	$250
Local, state taxes	+ 33
Total monthly cost	$283

The difference in the example is $24 in favor of the apartment, not a significant amount, especially considering that you can expect eventually to recover most of your $50,000 investment in a condo by reselling.

Another factor to look at is the possibility that one has more amenities than the other. And if you consider that in an apartment the rent can be raised, you must offset that by the expectation that there will be extra assessments for repair and replacement in a condo. There's one other item to think about: apartments are sometimes converted into condos. Renters must receive due notice, and, of course, can move out instead of buying.

The conclusions you can make from this example are that the fees being charged for the condo and the rent for the apartment seem to be equivalent and the price for the unit, therefore, reasonable. For a more detailed analysis, consult an accountant.

You will receive a mind-boggling set of papers when you arrange to buy a condo. They're beyond the ordinary layman and even lawyers not versed in real estate law. Smart buyers will search out a knowledgeable lawyer to explain what they contemplate signing by asking for guidance from the local bar association.

One of these papers by law has to be an offering circular which discloses the terms of the sale, describes the property involved, and makes a detailed estimate of the expenses to be expected. Remember that the latter is no guarantee of the fees that may be charged in the future, for inflation in costs is likely and depreciation of buildings and equipment is a fact of life.

Here are some tips for a wise buyer to consider:

> Be skeptical of come-ons.
> Read all the material.
> Know the rules and regulations.
> Consult a lawyer, appraiser, accountant.
> Think it over for a few days.
> Bargain for a good price.
> Don't accept oral promises.
> Don't accept evasive answers.
> Look at the surroundings.
> Observe the maintenance workers.
> Check premises for cleanliness and repairs.
> Ask for a record of past increases.

Talk to association officers.

Be sure you understand the easement restrictions.

Determine whether the site is vulnerable to wind and
flood damage.

If the condominium is incomplete, be careful. The developer may have overreached himself and may not be able to finish the job. What then would your investment be worth? Understand that you might have the bad luck or bad timing to face an unanticipated assessment shortly after you close.

When you sign a contract to buy, it's usual to put 10% down. If you're going to try to get a mortgage, have it stated in writing that in case you can't get one, your deposit will be returned. Also, take all your papers with you to the loan officer; he or she may have good advice for you. On the closing date sign the purchase papers and the mortgage and receive back a deed, an accounting, and a policy covering title insurance.

You have 15 days of grace in which you can withdraw from the deal. This right of waiver is guaranteed by the Condominium Law.

Obligations of a unit owner

Included in your monthly fee are the following expenses for the common elements: security, management, taxes, utilities, refuse services, lawn care, maintenance and repair, the use of recreational facilities, insurance, administrative expenses, salaries of workers, and amounts for reserves and depreciation.

This last item is an important safeguard required by law. It keeps down the amount that has to be assessed each member in case of a major repair bill that has suddenly surfaced. It can't give full protection against disasters, but insurance coverage should cushion them. There isn't much anybody can do about inflation.

You must be philosophical about assessments. Many hard feelings can grow out of these matters. The homeowners association is required by law to maintain the property and must do so even though it may not please all the members.

For example, suppose the roof of a multi-storied building needed repairs. Only the residents on the top floor were suffering from the leaky roof, but everyone had to pay his percentage share of the required repairs. Not only that, but the money would be needed promptly, for the contractor couldn't wait for the job to be finished to meet his payroll. Any member not paying his share is liable to have a lien placed on his unit.

Please note, too, that although part of your monthly fee covers insurance on the common elements of the condominium, you must insure your own furnishings and other personal property stored on the premises or in your unit. A special policy is offered to condo unit owners, covering hazards and damages in or out of the unit, personal property, fire and wind damage, theft, and vandalism. As is common, the coverages do not apply to anyone subletting your property.

Another obligation of the condo owner is to obey the rules. They are agreed to by inference when they are given to a member before he buys his unit. They're restrictive, but they protect you as well as control you. These are the kinds of rules to expect:

> qualifications for prospective buyers of your
>   property
> restrictions on your guests
> parking restrictions
> restrictions on decor that is visible outside
> maintenance of heating and cooling systems and
>   plumbing in your unit
> additional fees for certain facilities
> limitations on activities that disturb others
> control on subletting
> age restrictions on occupants, if legal.

A pertinent comment for buyers considering the purchase of a condominium was given in 1975 by the 4th District Court of Appeals in its decision on *Hidden Harbor Estates, Inc. v. Norman,* (309 So. 2s. 179). Here is an excerpt from that decision:

"Inherent in the condominium concept is the principle that to promote the health, happiness, and peace of mind of the majority of the unit owners, since they are living in such close proximity and using facilities in common, [is that] each unit owner must give up a certain degree of freedom of choice which he might otherwise enjoy in separate, privately owned property."

The association and its officers

The administration of the affairs of the condominium falls on a board of directors and its officers elected by members of the homeowners association, which includes all unit owners in the condominium. The association must be incorporated and is strictly regulated by Statutes 718. Meetings of the officers must be open to all members, and formal notice must be given of these meetings. Individual unit owners cannot act for the association without being empowered by the directors. And those who handle money must be bonded.

The board has power to buy and sell, make assessments, sign contracts, and the right at a reasonable time to enter units for the purpose of making repairs necessary to the structure of the building. The board buys insurance and keeps records which are subject to auditing and must be open to inspection at reasonable times by all members. Bylaws are made by the membership with the usual provisions adopted by such bodies: establishing a quorum, outlining the duties of the officers and the means of their recall, provision for amendment, requirements for calling meetings and elections.

The Southeast Region is "condo country," and the officers of the associations there are active politically, well organized, and vocal in proclaiming their rights.

There is one more item that needs explanation. If the condominium unit you own is a mobile home, it falls under Florida Statutes 723, but the provisions are basically the same as those for condominiums in FS 718.

After all these injunctions, you might want to stay as far away as you can from condominium living. Remember, though, that more than 2.5 million Floridians live in them. The units are usually pleasant and up-to-date, and the buildings are substantial. If you don't want to move into a building that you share in common with others, maybe you should look into the townhouse or cluster home variety. In them and in mobile home parks which belong to the residents, you do indeed own the exterior and roof of your dwelling. Most likely the fees will be lower, too, for there is less property held in common, although in single and cluster units you may be responsible for your share in the upkeep of the streets, which is an unlikely expense in a highrise. Please note another facet in favor of separate residences: resales are often easier and more profitable.

But if you value your independence more than the "comfort" of having your property taken care of, the next chapter about a site-built house on your own lot, may be what you're looking for.

8. Single Family Homes

Although single family homes might not be the first choice among retirees, they make up the bulk of the housing market. *The Florida Almanac, 1988-89,* reports single family homes have 65.5% of the residents; apartments have 24.9%, and mobile homes have 9.6% of the market.

If there weren't other considerations—such as maintenance, initial cost, recreational facilities, and companionship—most retirees would prefer the freedom of owning their own single homes. But retirees have been in the mainstream, are aware of the advantages and disadvantages, and have the know-how to make a personal choice.

What's the cost?

One of the first questions a retiree is likely to ask is how the prices of homes in Florida compare with those of the rest of the country. Four Florida cities are represented among the most expensive metropolitan markets, according to figures published by the National Association of Realtors for the end of 1987. The median price of resale homes is highest in New York at $180,800; Palm Beach is tenth at $103,200; Miami/Hialeah is 17th at $80,300; and Orlando is 20th at $78,600.

For the purchase of new homes in 1985, based on mortgages issued, these were listed in the *Florida Statistical Almanac:*

> Daytona Beach, $71,300
> Fort Lauderdale/Hollywood, $96,700
> Fort Myers/Cape Coral, $93,200
> Gainesville, $92,800
> Jacksonville, $101,100
> Lakeland/Winter Haven, $75,600
> Melbourne/Cocoa, $82,900
> Miami, $99,000
> Orlando, $102,700
> Pensacola, $82,300
> Sarasota, $95,900
> Tallahassee, $83,400
> Tampa/St. Petersburg, $85,100
> West Palm Beach/Boca Raton, $96,800

Characteristics

Conventional homes in Florida have some differences from those in the North. The majority of them are one story, and almost all have a screened room attached. The heating and air conditioning systems are usually in the same unit, and both operate through ducts that carry the heated or cooled air. It's extremely rare to find a Florida house with a cellar. The pipes that carry water from, and wastes to the mains are plastic, and nobody worries particularly if portions of them are exposed, as they're unlikely to freeze.

Except for varieties of limestone, there is no rock for building in Florida. Sometimes you'll find homes faced with simulated stone, but the real thing is rare. The basic modest home is constructed of cinderblock that is painted, stuccoed, or faced with brick or stone sheathing. If it's not made of cinderblock, it will be constructed of wood and shingled with wood, synthetics, or aluminum.

Single home in a small town in Florida, ideal for retirees.

Clermont Realty, Inc.

Househunting hints

If you've found a house with all the amenities you want, don't let the stars in your eyes blind you to possible defects. Before you sign the papers for a resale home, hire a licensed appraiser to look at the working parts: the wiring, the stability, the foundation, the plumbing, the roof, the windows and doors, any water damage, the heating/cooling element, insulation, etc. It will cost you $200, more or less, for his services, but it can easily save you ten times that much. Ask him to take you along on his inspection. Inquire whether he makes any guarantee, and check whether he has done a termite inspection.

If it's a new home, see what warranty the builder offers. At a minimum it should be to fix anything that is his responsibility for a year, and on some important systems for longer periods.

Whether you buy a previously-owned home or a new one, you might like to make the careful examination suggested in Chapter 5 under the subheading "Setting up the mobile home."

There's a list of questions to ask concerning possible neighborhood and environmental problems.

Talk to the neighbors about occurrences of vandalism and burglaries. See how the highways are between you and the nearest supermarket, the post office, the library, your church, a shopping mall, medical attention, and fire and police protection. Ask at city hall whether any changes are anticipated, like road improvements, new sewer systems, or public projects that could disrupt your peace.

Protection from the elements

When you're buying or building your home, the first consideration should be the vulnerability of the site to flooding. Please check with the nearest water management district or city hall to see whether the location you like is on a floodplain, and if it is, how it's designated. Is it prone to flooding in just a heavy rainy season, or is it likely to be flooded only once in an average of 25 years by a hurricane? Is the main floor of the house raised well above ground level and on the highest portion of the lot? Is the house near the ocean or on the shore of a lake? For a better understanding of the possibilities of flooding, please refer to Chapter 10, The Endangered Environment.

Generally speaking, the walls of cinderblock houses are hurricane-resistant. The roofs and the windows, carports and utility buildings are not. A few measures will help. First, be sure the carport roof is not integrated with the house roof. Wind that can lift off the carport roof could take an attached house roof along with it. Aluminum awnings that can be lowered to cover the windows are a convenient way to protect the glass and also serve to keep out the rain. Utility buildings can be tied down with reinforcements or built of cinderblock. Remember that coastal areas, including the Panhandle, receive the brunt of hurricanes. Land masses slow them down, so that inland areas aren't so often hit as coastal areas. However, the violence of hurricanes can devastate central Florida as well. Except for a small area on the Georgia border, no part of the state is more than 60 miles from a coast. Even if you never need the protection outlined above, you can feel secure having it. While you're checking on the floodplain at city hall, ask about their emergency plans for windstorms.

You can't protect yourself from tornadoes. They're local phenomena and they occur everywhere on this level land. Tornadoes are different from ordinary high winds because they create vacuums that so that the higher internal pressure can cause a structure to explode. All you can do is hope for favorable odds and pay your insurance premiums.

Trees can provide you with excellent protection against the brutal summer sun. You're lucky if you can find a home with sound, mature trees. They can blow down on a house in fierce winds, so be sure there's a margin between the house and the trees. Trunks can do more serious damage than branches. If your lot doesn't have this natural air conditioning, you can at least see that the roof is gabled to provide a buffer and that the structure is painted in white or light colors.

Building wisely

If you plan to have your house built for you, you have a chance to eliminate some problems that could later plague you. In the matter of heat control, in addition to the trees and the light paint suggested above, you can orient your house in the manner suggested by architects and builders. Have it placed on an east-west axis with the major living areas facing south. To allow for less heat exchange on the eastern and western ends, favor smaller windows placed high.

You might like to consider building a home with the rooms forming a perimeter about a central patio, Spanish style, or one patterned after the old Cracker houses. Cracker houses were built with cross ventilation on all four sides, raised above the ground for air circulation underneath, and had surrounding roofed porches to allow the windows to remain open during rainstorms.

(The word "Cracker" as applied to this area of the country often has a pejorative connotation. Its origin, however, was

Florida styling and minimum upkeep are featured in single family home.

Matsche Realty Co.

respectable enough, for it was first used to describe the cattle ranchers who cracked whips while herding their stock to market.)

Even if you don't want to "go native" to the extent suggested above, with the proper placing of windows and doors you can provide a cross breeze. The prevailing winds are east and southeast. Remember that before the end of World War II all home air conditioning was "natural."

A covered verandah not only lets in the breeze and keeps out the rain, but it will permit the winter sun, which is lower in the sky, to help warm your house. This use of natural forces to enhance your heating and cooling systems is called passive energy. It can save you a great deal of money, for heating and cooling account for 53% of your electric usage, according to Florida Power Corporation.

A pitched roof is an advantage. You won't need it for shedding a load of snow, but it will give you a bigger attic space and room for extra insulation to help your climate control. R-19 is the recommended rating for attic insulation, but you can go much higher. If you shingle the roof, ask the builder to provide mildew-resistant shingles, or you may find them turning black with fungus in a few years.

Even locating closets on the exterior walls of a home helps control heat and cold. A well-designed fireplace is a help. A heat pump is recommended as a very effective way to fight cold weather as well as the heat of summer. Don't forget to use overhead or portable fans, too. You can set your thermostat much higher in hot weather if you place fans opposite each other across an area where there is a reasonably straight line.

A few other tips to consider: a frame house is cooler than one of concrete block; double paned and tinted windows filter out heat or cold; window awnings help keep out bright sun; and skylights let in heat along with light, so don't use them just for show—they belong on an atrium or in a room with no other source of light.

If you require air conditioning when it's just too hot or someone in your home suffers from allergies, you will probably find comfort in a setting between 78 and 80 degrees. Florida Power Corporation sent its consumers a table of the costs of different settings of the thermostat. The costs, of course, reflect the amount of energy consumed.

Thermostat Set At	Costs
80 degrees	save 16%
79	save 8%
78	
77	increase 8%
76	increase 18%
75	increase 28%
74	increase 39%
73	increase 50%

There are two systems to consider to cut down on the cost and increase the efficiency of heating hot water, which accounts for 17% of electric consumption. One is to install a solar heater. It's best done when the house is being built. The other is to use waste heat recovery from your air conditioner. The latter is less efficient and isn't useful all year-round, but it requires less complicated installation.

Using simple and natural controls does more than just save money. It's healthier and environmentally safer. Besides, growth has led to unavoidable power shortages and more and more dependence on nuclear energy. You're doing your bit to preserve the quality of life of your new state.

One more suggestion will give you a degree of peace of mind in this uncertain world. When your house is being built, have a security system added. It can range from a protected entry with a "bullhorn" placed out of reach, or an infrared sensing device inside, to "complete" protection with steel doors and with windows outlined with sensors. Perhaps nothing can stop a professional burglar, but you don't have to make it easy for him.

A very helpful publication for building or buying your retirement home is issued by the state. It's entitled *Housing Solutions for Florida Seniors—a "how-to" manual*, and is co-published by the Florida Department of Community Affairs and the Miami Jewish Home and Hospitals for the Aged, Inc. The address of the Department is 2571 Executive Center Circle, East Tallahassee, Fl 32301.

Care of the grounds

You have better things to do than fertilize, weed, trim, and mow the lawn. Pick out as small a lot as you need for privacy, and then replace some of the lawn with ground cover. A listing of some of these is found in Chapter 11, Growing Things. A row of pine trees along the lot line will provide its own buffer of fallen needles and the bonus of a sweet smell.

Concrete or tarmac are not the only materials you can use for a driveway. Aggregates and mulches do a better job in several ways. They don't reflect heat; they allow the rainwater to flow naturally into the aquifer; they're pleasanter to walk on. Use them, or commercial stepping stones, for your walkways, as well. If you're making a terrace, try loosely laid bricks.

Hibiscus, poinsettias, camellias, and other exotics, which are too tender for the Northern winters, entice the novice Floridian. You can grow them almost anywhere in the state, but in the northern and central regions you may have to cover them against a predicted frost. Wrap them in discarded blankets or a tent of heavy plastic. Mulch the roots well. If the frost is severe, you can try a low-wattage electric bulb under a tent cover. Chances are that if the leaves fall, the root will still be intact, and you can prune away the dead wood at a later date. Unless you're a dedicated gardener, when the novelty has worn off, you may wish to plant evergreens and hardy shrubs instead.

If you build or buy on a waterfront, there are some hints to help preserve the banks, the water, and your property. Your main objective should be to slow runoff water as the best way to preserve the natural boundaries and "lifestyle" of the body of water. One way to do this is to contour the surface of the land in an undulating pattern with the "waves" parallel to the shoreline. These alternate rises (called berms) and dips (called swales) hold the rainwater, allowing it to seep into the aquifer instead of running into the lake. Terracing performs a similar function.

Another way to help nature is to allow the native vegetation to remain at the edge of the water. Don't try to confine a lake with a "sea wall." Don't drive your boat fast enough near shore to make a strong wake. Don't use artificial pesticides, especially chlorinated hydrocarbons and organic phosphates. Try organic controls and fertilizers that decay to enrich the soil.

Moving in

Regardless of whether or not you bring your furniture, you're going to want to bring enough personal effects to warrant dragging a rented hauler behind the family car. Consider a number of things before you decide to move all your household goods:

1.   The cost of buying new furniture.   Your new furnishings will probably be cheaper in Florida than they would be in your Northern home because the lifestyle is more casual, but it's probably not as cheap as moving.

2.   How important your present pieces are.   Would you like to give your heirlooms and collections away to your children or friends before you go to the trouble of moving them? Do you

have some solid wood furniture that is worth a lot more than today's pressed wood/synthetic grain construction? Have you items you consider indispensable or irreplaceable?

3.   The cost of moving.   The nationwide movers have to conform to U.S. law, which makes their prices nearly uniform. They do an efficient job of marking and listing each piece. You can help yourself by making your own inventory. (You can put it in the safe deposit box with your records later.) Also, it helps to mark each box with its contents, the number of the bill of lading, your name, and the room into which it will go.

The prices below are quoted for early 1988, but have risen only a few dollars since 1980. They include basic insurance. There are extra charges for pieces, like pianos, that require special handling. The 1,200 miles represents the distance from Kansas City to Central Florida, and the 1,000 from Philadelphia. Six rooms of furniture will probably have a net weight between 4,000 and 8,000 pounds.

Distance in miles	2,000 lb.	4,000 lb.	8,000 lb.
1,000	$685	$1,048	$1,788
1,200	740	1,132	1,944

It pays to have the mover pack your china, floor lamps, mirrors, mattresses, microwave ovens, stereo equipment and television sets. Forms will be provided for you to make claims for damage, and if you're especially cautious, you can follow the truck to the weighing station to verify that you're being charged for the exact weight of your furniture.

4.   The practicality of do-it-yourself moving.   If you're sure you and your helping friends or hired workers won't damage electronic equipment and other fragile pieces in loading or transporting, you may save money by renting a moving truck. The cost for a 24-foot truck for six days to drive 1,000 miles to a Florida destination is about $1,700. It's especially high because more people drive into the state than leave it, and there's the added expense to the company of paying a driver to return the truck. If you hire one locally, the cost is $40 a day plus $.35 a mile.

Carry your own small valuables with you in your car—camera, radios, jewelry, medicines, family albums, and records. If you're worried about theft en route, you can have a friend or family member send small valuables to you by express mail once you're in your new home.

Ongoing expenses

There are factors that make the cost of living lower in Florida. Probably the major one is the savings on fuel, for even if the argument is made that the cost of air conditioning offsets the cost of heating, there are still at least six months of the year when people in good health need neither. Then there's the casual outdoor living that makes for lighter meals and leisure clothing. Your home will not be subject to possible damage by ice and snow. Your furniture and your house will need cleaning less often, for the exchange of air clears away dust particles, and any sand that might be brought in is easier to clean up than mud would be. Taxes are lower, partly because of the income from tourism.

There's no promise that all these costs will remain favorable. Taxes, for example, are soaring because of the need to build roads and schools, to add new police and firemen, to build the infrastructure to support all the new housing. Cries are going up from the taxpayers to increase the impact fees on new housing. This is one argument for buying a resale home.

For whatever significance it may have, here are the yearly expenses for 1987 for a four-bedroom, two-and-a-half-bath, 1,700-square-foot, energy-efficient home in Tampa:

property and school taxes (including exemption)	$ 972
hazard insurance	329
electricity	972
water and sewer	444
sanitation	84
	$2,769

Be sure you have flood and wind coverage in your hazard insurance. Florida residents buy more flood insurance than residents of any other state. Louisiana is a distant second. There are areas of the state in which the federal government mandates flood insurance for all homes on which it issues mortgages. For a $70,000 home the average cost is $260 a year. The coverage, under an arm of the Federal Emergency Management Agency, loses money nearly every year at those rates.

If you have your own home on your own lot in fee simple, you can build a fence, have pets, entertain guests without restrictions, plant a garden, and enjoy your independence. If zoning laws permit, you can build a garage or storage building, enclose a porch, make an addition, paint the house any color you wish. You don't need to lack companionship, either, for everywhere in Florida there are clubs and services for retired people.

Every kind of housing has its own benefits and drawbacks. Chapter 9, which follows, takes a look at apartments and different types of congregate living facilities.

9. *Apartments and Assisted Living*

A quarter of the housing in the state is in the form of apartments. In 1986, according to the *Florida Statistical Almanac*, there were 16,148 apartment buildings containing more than half a million units. Not included in the tabulation were rental condominiums, time-share tenancies, transient apartments in hotels and motels, and those with units of fewer than five.

The greatest number of units are in the most populous counties:

Dade-Broward-Palm Beach (Southeast)
Pinellas-Hillsborough-Sarasota (West)
Orange-Volusia (Central)
Duval (Northeast)
Escambia-Bay (Panhandle)

Before you move into an apartment, read the lease. Be sure everything you're promised is down there in black and white. Be sure you understand your obligations. Pay attention to any limitations on rent increases, and if there aren't any, ask for a list of increases that have been made in the past.

Advantages of apartments

Apartments are great for those who want the option open to move away with relative ease if they decide to live elsewhere. They're fine for people who might be transferred. And for retirees who aren't sure they can stay far from their old friends.

They're especially good for people who aren't able or are too busy to take care of maintenance. It's great to pick up the phone and call the manager to send someone to fix your leaky faucet. Other things are taken care of, too, such as phone and cable TV outlets. Services such as trash pickup and water and sewer use are usually included in the rent. A thermostat that operates at the spin of a dial is much easier to live with than a heating and air conditioning system you have to maintain. Pay your rent and your electric and phone bills and the insurance on your furnishings, and forget about the rest of the expenses of keeping up a home.

Apartment houses often offer recreational and social activities. Large complexes have swimming pools, exercise rooms, social rooms, tennis courts, and shuffleboard. That gives a tenant a chance to meet his neighbors.

They provide some security for tenants. Not only are incoming guests screened, either by security personnel or by tenant control of an electronic device, but the proximity of fellow tenants in neighboring apartments is a safety measure. You can leave for vacation at any time without worrying about a house and lawn while you're gone.

Often apartment buildings are centrally located, allowing tenants to keep the car in the garage or the parking space provided while they walk to shops and entertainment.

Except for the consideration you show for others in the building, you can do as you please in your apartment. There may be restrictions on pets and certain nuisances that bother your neighbors, but usually you can have as many guests as you can accommodate, as often as you wish.

When you rent an apartment, you can keep your savings invested to earn interest to pay the rent or to spend as you wish. If you need cash in a hurry, it's available, whereas if you've put it into the equity in a house, you might have to borrow on the equity or sell the property first. That could take time, and besides, you could lose money on the deal. If you finance the purchase of a home, there's also the likelihood that your mortgage payments would exceed the rental charges for a comparable apartment.

It's hard to determine the average rent for an apartment. There are too many factors: location, amenities, amount of floorspace, number of units in the building, and changing market conditions. In an overbuilt urban area in central Florida in early 1988, one in which the rent levels were slightly depressed, an efficiency or a one-bedroom, one-bath apartment rented from $350 to $400; a 2/1 went for about $450; a 2/2 close to $500; and a 3/2 for $550 or more.

Disadvantages of apartments

Of course, renting lacks some advantages of home ownership. There is the leverage of the owner's home in case he has to borrow money. That makes the equity comparable to money in the bank. If the home appreciates in value, that's a plus, for at the same time one can expect the monthly rental for apartments to rise. One property insurance company which researched the appreciation of values in single houses reported that between 1972 and 1987 there was an average 8.1% annual increase in market value. Inflation was high for part of that period, however, and that's no indication of any future appreciation.

There is the saving in taxes with the homestead exemption. Also, there is the one-time exclusion of capital gains up to $125,000 allowed by the Internal Revenue Service when a person 55 or older sells his principal residence. If he sells his replacement home subsequently, he can defer taxation on the profit through the rollover replacement rule.

If a renter is disillusioned or if he has a change of some kind in his life that requires him to move, it might not be so easy to leave his apartment. Leases usually run for a year, which means the rent won't go up during that period, but which also obliges a tenant to stay that long or in some cases find a replacement.

Not the least advantage to the homeowner is his freedom from the restrictions that come from sharing a dwelling place with others. A man's home, as they say, is his castle.

There's another potential danger that threatens apartment dwellers. Apartment houses are sometimes converted into condominiums, in which case the tenant must either buy his space or move out. Unless the lease states otherwise, the tenant has 180 days to move after he receives the notice of conversion by registered mail. If his lease would expire before the 180 prescribed days, he can ask for an extension if he notifies the developer within thirty days. If he decides to buy a condo unit, he is entitled to an inspection report of the common elements in which he will hold an interest. A cautious prospective owner can hire his own inspector.

Congregate living facilities

"Congregate living" has really two meanings. Generically, it means a group of people living together; specifically it means a certain kind of group living with minimal extra care for the individuals sharing the arrangements. In the title of this section the generic meaning is employed.

Congregate living comes in three principal categories, with some variations among these. The first is a residential care facility. This arrangement is for senior citizens who are elderly but still active. The official classification is Adult Congregate Living Facility, known as an ACLF. Regulation of these homes is by the Florida Department of Health and Rehabilitative Services. In them the residents receive room, board, and small personal services, such as help in dressing.

The second type is classified as Continuing Care and Rehabilitative Community, or CCRC. These provide rooms or separate housing, board, and some care in a nursing facility.

The third is a nursing home, designed for those who need round-the-clock care. As in a hospital, private and semiprivate rooms are available. It's for confused or incapacitated people.

Residential care

An estimated 1,500 adult congregate living facilities (ACLFs) are found in the state. Sometimes they're called "assisted living services." They permit personal freedom with the security of a call button in case a resident has a problem. Nursing services are minimal: dispensing medication that has been prescribed, taking blood pressure, calling your doctor. Usually they provide small apartments, villas, or cluster homes, one or more meals, linen service, maid service, utilities, and some recreational activities. They may be built as an adjunct to a nursing home.

Depending on the degree of luxury or services provided, the costs of these living arrangements range from about $400 a month to $2,000, according to the Department of Health and Rehabilitative Services. If you're ready for this life style, or if you still have the responsibility of an aged parent when you retire and you don't know where to look, you can get a current list of ACLFs for $20. Make your check payable to the State of Florida, and send it to The Florida Department of Health and Rehabilitative Services, ACLF Program, 2727 Mahan Drive, Tallahassee, FL 32308.

This is the least expensive of the three facilities, but its services aren't for those who need more comprehensive care. At any time the need arises, a resident can be moved into another facility and even returned when he has recovered. This is particularly convenient if the ACLF is part of a complex that includes a nursing home.

Before you move in or arrange to enter someone else, please consult the Better Business Bureau. Look at the kind and quantity of the food served; see what the linens provided are like; ask how rates may change; observe the cleanliness and maintenance of the building and grounds; talk to the present residents; and if you wish, send for this booklet: *Home, Your Choice: A Workbook for Older People and Their Families,* issued by the American Association of Retired Persons. Address: AARP Fulfillment Unit, P.O. Box 2240, Long Beach, Ca, 90810.

Continuing care

At the time this book was written there were 67 Continuing Care and Rehabilitative Communities in the state. To find the current listing, please write to the Florida Department of Insurance, Bureau of Allied Lines, Room 637, Larson Building, Tallahassee, Fl 32301.

You make a financial commitment when you move into a CCRC. It's in the form of a substantial fee related to the living quarters you choose. The average entrance fee is $80,000 but can go to $200,000. One or two persons can move in for this fee. The monthly charge ranges from $400 to $1,500 for the first occupant and an additional amount (half or less) for the second.

For the monthly charges you will receive security, parking space, maid service, linens, daily meal(s), activities, scheduled transportation, 24-hour emergency nursing service, therapy and recuperative care in a skilled nursing facility for a limited number of days, and assisted living when necessary. *For life.*

You will be given a contract to sign for this one, for you occupy, although you don't own, a piece of property. That means that if the CCRC folds, you have no claim to the property even though you paid the entrance fee. Of course, you need to read the contract carefully, take it to your lawyer or accountant, and talk it over with your family, but here's what is of particular concern:

How much can the monthly charge be raised?

Is there any return of the entrance fee when you die or give up the living quarters?

How many days of skilled nursing care are you allowed?

What extra charges can be made?

What are the meals like, and can you have a special diet?

One of the most important matters to consider is what disposition is made of the initial investment. In some CCRCs, such as church-run institutions, where the entrance fee is modest, the amount refundable if the resident dies or moves away diminishes to zero over the course of five or six years. In commercial, for-profit establishments the payback can be on a sliding scale, a stated amount such as 50%, or even some figure close to 100%. In the meantime, of course, the company has profited by the income derived from the fee, and upon the withdrawal of the resident, it can find a replacement to occupy the living quarters that have been given up.

Another consideration is the size of the living quarters provided. These range from studio size to two bedroom two bath apartments, cluster homes, or villas. The monthly charges vary with these facilities, and sometimes the initial fee does, too. In one apartment style CCRC, the number of square feet in the units ranged from 528 to 1256. Villas or cluster homes in other communities averaged slightly larger.

Check on the health care section of a CCRC. Ask to be shown the facilities and inquire about the medical qualifications of the staff.

Even though the salesman-consultant is friendly and helpful and doesn't intend to deceive you, don't accept oral promises. Written commitments are proof, words aren't.

Be especially careful to evaluate a facility you like. These are usually large developments. According to the AARP, ten percent of CCRCs nationwide have either folded or been in financial trouble. Because of the straits in which residents of these communities found themselves—their fees lost and their provision for lifetime care gone—the Florida Department of Insurance now requires a large percentage of the monies from the entrance fees to be placed in an escrow fund until the development has sufficient occupancy and is considered by the agency to be fiscally sound to use the funds for additional construction.

The American Association of Homes for the Aging (AAHA), which represents 95% of the nonprofit continuing care facilities, can supply without charge a list of those it has accredited. Write to the AAHA, 1129 20th Street, NW, Suite 400, Washington, DC 20036.

Florida is one of the fourteen states that regulate these two types of retirement housing. If you'd like to read the text of the statutes, you can request copies from the agencies in charge. The ACLFs are covered under Chapter 400, and the CCRCs under Chapter 651.

Nursing homes

There are 500 nursing homes, serving 54,000 residents, in the state. They provide private and semiprivate rooms for people recovering from surgery after they have left a hospital or for those who require 24-hour attention because of their inability to care for themselves. Half of the patients in this situation have Alzheimer's disease. The homes must be licensed by the Department of Health and Rehabilitative Services, from which a list can be ordered. Write to the HRS, Office of Licensure and Certification, 2727 Mahan Drive, Tallahassee, Fl 32308.

The cost per day ranges from $45 to $115 in those institutions that qualify as skilled nursing care facilities covered by Medicare, according to the Florida Health Care Association. Medicare coverage was expanded by the Catastrophic Health Insurance Act of 1988, effective January 1, 1989. After a co-payment of 20% for the first eight days of skilled nursing home care, Medicare picks up the tab to a total of 150 days a year. Supplementary insurance can cover some of the excess costs or days of care, depending on the specifications of the different policies.

Please note that a skilled nursing facility offers acute care while a custodial nursing home offers long-term care. The custodial care is not covered under the act. To understand what is and is not covered, you can write for the Health Care Financing Administration's "Guide to Health Insurance for People with Medicare." Single copies may be obtained from HCFA, Consumer Information Center, P.O. Box 100, Pueblo, CO 81002.

When a patient's medical coverage is exhausted, his or her spouse is responsible for any further payments. The average cost of a year's stay is $22,000, and the average stay is 456 days. Before this law was enacted, a spouse was often left destitute in an effort to pay for such care, but new provisions allow the spouse to keep half the couple's assets and an income of $786 a month. Medicaid takes over any costs that would reduce the spouse's assets below these amounts.

Additional benefits are phased in over a period of five years. These include drugs and hospice and home care within limits. The amount of income a spouse can keep for his own needs also escalates.

The Medicare coverages listed here change from time to time. To learn what new provisions are, contact the nearest office of the Social Security Administration from the listing in the phone book.

Be extremely careful in buying an insurance policy to cover nursing home care. An overview and a comparative study of nursing homes, entitled "Who Can Afford a Nursing Home?", appeared in *Consumer Reports Magazine* for May, 1988. From its studies it concluded that many policies are vague and quirky and provide inadequate coverage. If the article isn't available or timely when you're considering nursing home care, write to Health and Human Services for up-to-date information. The address is Health and Human Services, Health Care Financing Administration, 200 Independence Avenue SW, Washington DC 20201.

An alternative, if the patient is not extremely ill, is worth consideration: home health care. Admittedly, this places a tremendous burden on the person responsible for the care, but it may also be better for the patient. To assist the caretaker, beginning in 1990 Medicare pays for the services of a skilled nurse or home health aide for a limited number of days. In addition to this at-home care, visiting nurses are provided by state agencies like Health and Rehabilitative Services.

Adult day-care centers and hired "sitters" can also take off some of the stress. Volunteers from senior citizens' organizations often help with services to the caretaker.

There have been some tragic instances of the abuse of elderly patients in nursing homes. Even in the best institutions there can be problems, for staff workers have demanding jobs and comparatively low pay. If someone close to you is in a nursing home, visit often at different times to observe his care firsthand. Your presence, however brief, can have a good psychological effect on the patient.

In response to abuses and complaints, the HRS is asking the state legislature for tighter controls on the homes and for more money to increase the number of inspectors it can send into the field.

Every kind of housing you look into has problems. It's no different from the rest of life. Your choice is always a compromise. Yet many people are enjoying their retirement in each kind of housing we've looked at, except the unfortunate ones in nursing homes. Life is a little easier in Florida, but in the end, it's not where you live, but who you are, that ultimately determines your happiness.

Let's conclude our look at housing, and turn to the next three chapters for the physical characteristics of the land and for the plants and animals that share it with us for the time we're here.

10. The Endangered Environment

Today every thinking person is aware that we live in an endangered world. Overpopulation is outdistancing the food supply; irreplaceable resources are being depleted; air and land and sea are polluted; the social fabric is strained by crime and disease; and now scientists tell us there's a hole in the sky!

So, if you read in this chapter that Florida's fair land is threatened by man's greed, natural disasters, and the increasing piles of waste from a throwaway society, you'll be able to put it into perspective as a microcosm of what's happening throughout the world. Except that Florida's ecology is more fragile than most, and what's happening all around us may be happening faster here.

How Florida began

Once, they say, there was only one land form, Pangaea. From this giant continent all the land masses of the present world gradually separated. As the continent known as North America moved to its present position, it gradually took on new contours:

bays and river estuaries, offshore islands and capes emerged. Geologically the last part to form was the low-lying peninsula known as Florida.

The state is situated on the land portion of the Floridian Plateau, a continuation of the Appalachian range that runs down the Eastern seaboard. The Plateau is 500 miles or so long and between 250 and 400 miles wide. The water-covered portion makes a shelf of shallow depth in the Atlantic and the Gulf of Mexico before it drops off into deep water. On the Atlantic side the continental shelf is narrower than on the Gulf side because it's worn by the high energy waves of that ocean. The shelf is igneous and metamorphic rock that evolved from the heating and cooling of the earth. Outcroppings of the base rock run parallel to the coast.

Upon this base lies 4,000 feet—four-fifths of a mile—of sedimentary rock, chiefly limestone (calcium carbonate), laid down during the Eocene epoch. Overlying the limestone is clay from the Miocene Epoch, and on top of that is sand from the Pleistocene epoch. They make up the land area of the state.

It's believed the sea was once 270 feet above its present level, cutting off the entire state. So low is the profile of Florida that if the sea were to rise only 50 feet, half the state would be under water. So shallow are the shelves on either side that if the sea were to drop 50 feet, a third more land would be added.

While the land was inundated, it was home to many sea creatures. They lived out their life span and dropped their skeletal remains to the floor beneath them. The limestone from their shells was built up over many millenia until it solidified into a porous rock. If you look at pieces of the limestone base that underlies the sands, you will see the fossilized remains of early sea life.

Over the limestone layer is a crust of soil. Most of it is sand, which drains away moisture and nutrients. The low hills have layers of clay, and in some areas there is a rich, black, organic soil called muck, which accounts for the fine multi-season vegetables grown in the state. It was laid down like oil deposits from the bodies of animals and dead plants.

More than 700,000 acres of muck are to be found around the perimeter of the Everglades; about 10,000 more are found near Lake Apopka in Central Florida. Close to Lake Okeechobee the muck is as deep as 18 feet, but it's as shallow as two feet in other areas. Muck is depleting at the rate of one or two inches a year. Measures to conserve it include reflooding, returning nutrients, especially by-products of sugar cane, and saving the best land for crops that demand it, using the marginal muckland for others.

Florida rose out of the sea, geologists say, 25 million years ago, just before the beginning of what is called the Miocene epoch. As soon as enough plants grew to support life, animals from the older parts of the continent moved in to make their homes. They were very different from the animals of today, but recognizable as their ancestors: rhinoceroses, tapirs, camels, horses, elephants, and giant members of the cat and dog families to prey upon them. There were amphibians and reptiles— turtles, alligators, lizards, snakes, and frogs—but these didn't change as much during the long geologic time.

By the time the Pliocene epoch began about 5 million years ago, Panama, the last section of Central America, was completed as a bridge between the continents of North and South America, and creatures from both places cross-migrated. Armadillos, opossums, and porcupines were among the arrivals from the south. When the Pliocene epoch eased into the Pleistocene, many large animals, like saber-toothed cats, jaguars, cave bears, mastodons, and camels, roamed the forests of Florida.

The Pleistocene epoch ended with the first of the four ice ages, which lasted until about 10,000 years ago. By the time the recent epoch began, many of the earlier animals were dead. Their remains are still discovered as fossils in excavations. Among those that survived this long history is the Florida panther, whose numbers today are said to be no more than thirty.

For a fascinating account of the early forms of life found in the state, read the richly illustrated book *Florida's Fossils* by Robin C. Brown, listed in the bibliography in the back pages of this book.

How the natural land is today

In, on, and above the land today live an astounding number of creatures. Some 80 species of mammals, a third of which are aquatic, are indigenous to Florida. Hundreds of species of birds, both migratory and native, can be found in the state. Half of all bird species occurring in the United States are found in Florida. Snakes, turtles, frogs and, of course, alligators make their homes here. Both freshwater and saltwater fish are found in plentiful supply and variety.

Most of the surface soil is sand, requiring frequent replacement of water and nutrients, which filter easily through it. In undeveloped land there are still stands of the trees that once formed the predominant cover: pine, palm, cypress, and oak. Along the coastline there are sandy beaches, saltwater marshes, and mangrove forests. Between 3,000 and 4,000 plants are native to Florida.

Surface water is found abundantly in the many rivers and lakes. The pattern of the flow of rivers is best understood by looking at a phenomenon known as the Green Swamp. This is an 870-square mile stretch of wetlands and islands in Central Florida, located in Polk and surrounding counties. Because it's the highest ground water, it serves as the watershed of the state. From it flow five principal rivers: Withlacoochee, Hillsboro, Peace, Kissimmee, and Oklawaha. Seventy percent of the water used in the state, which consumes 17 billion gallons a day, comes from the Green Swamp. It flows in seasonal highs and lows. The northward flow feeds creeks and rivers and lakes, some of which eventually join the St. Johns River. All the major springs of Florida are north of the Green Swamp. The lakes just above the swamp have desirable levels of 97 or 98 feet above sea level. Southward at Lake Okeechobee the South Florida Water

Management District likes to hold the lake to 15.5 feet above sea level before the hurricane season starts.

The aquifer

Aquifer is a word derived from two Latin roots meaning "water bearer." It's not a phenomenon special to Florida, but a term for the part of the structure of the landmass underneath the soil that retains ground water as clean and potable.

Florida ground water is held in two separate aquifers. The Floridan Aquifer (spelled without an "i"), which begins in Santa Rosa and Okaloosa Counties in the Western Panhandle, stretches as far as Lake Okeechobee in the south central part of the Peninsula. The second, called the Biscayne Aquifer, covers the southeast corner of the state, supplying the needs of the populous coastal area.

Lake Okeechobee covers 730 square miles, but its average depth is only 15 feet. After Lake Michigan it is the largest freshwater lake within the country. It drains 5,000 square miles of land through its principal tributary, the Kissimmee River. But it's not only a reservoir, for the overflow, controlled by dikes and canals on the south, provides water for agriculture, and feeds the wetlands of the Everglades.

Four canals begin in the lake: Miami, 81 miles; Caloosahatchee (to the Gulf), 69 miles; St. Lucie (to the Atlantic), 40 miles; Hillsboro (to Boca Raton), 52 miles.

After surface water has been cleansed in the swamps, marshes, and sandy soil on the surface, it flows in underground rivers through the layers of porous limestone. When a well is sunk, it taps this water.

When rainwater falls, it naturally does one of two things, runs off or soaks in. Man interrupts these processes to take an estimated 12% of the supply for his purposes. The aquifers presently receive about 21 billion gallons a day, mostly from wetlands and sandy soils. The remainder evaporates to fall in the next rain or to trickle into a river and flow into the sea.

The portion that soaks in passes through subsoil and rocks to the porous rock where it is retained. This *charges* the aquifers.

The natural beauty that surrounds Wakulla Springs near Tallahassee. It is the world's deepest natural spring.

When an aquifer thrusts upward to the surface of the land, it *discharges* water through springs. Florida is famous for these freshwater springs. The best known of these is Silver Springs, which discharges 530 million gallons daily of 99.76% pure water. A supply of 646,000 gallons a day, or one cubic foot per second, is enough to provide for the water requirements of 6,000 persons. Silver Springs discharges 800 times that much, or enough for 4,800,000 persons. (A list of the principal springs can be found in Appendix III.)

The level and motion of the underground water are complicated processes controlled by gravity, capillary action, volume of water, and porosity of rocks. The highest point to which water reaches is called the water table. The lowest levels of ground water contain salt from the intrusion of the ocean.

The greatest recharge of the Floridan Aquifer per square foot takes place in the lake country of Central Florida. As the coastal cities with a short water supply become overpopulated, they seek the fresh water resources in these counties. Water then becomes a regional and political football with short-term and long-term water conservation interests in conflict.

The real issue, though, that must be squarely faced is that more and more water is drawn out of the aquifers and less and less flows in. The blame falls on growth and development which cover the land surface with buildings, roads, shopping malls, and parking lots. Important recharge areas are drained as "useless" swamps to turn them into "valuable" land for development. This short-sighted approach is very gradually giving way to long-term planning. As a stopgap measure some municipalities require all new construction to provide troughs or ponds into which the runoff can drain, and hopefully find its way into the aquifer.

There's no use even to think of tapping into the pure and plentiful water in Florida's springs. To do so would substantially reduce the flow in rivers and eventually into estuaries. That would compound the ecological disaster.

Water contamination

When a lake is born from ground water or a spring, it's pure water. It is said to be oligotrophic; that is, it has few nutrients which cause plant growth to cloud its waters. Lakes in this condition are home to gamefish such as largemouth bass, bluegills, bream, and crappies.

Gradually, over a period of many years, a lake goes through a process called eutrophication, a word that comes from two Greek roots meaning "well nourished." Leaves fall into it, insects die in it, dead fish decay, bird droppings fall, and runoff from the surrounding land sheds organic matter into it. These all decay and form nutrients on the bottom of the lake. Eventually aquatic weeds have a base for growth, and fish of different species find a home there: shad, gar, and catfish are characteristic. As the plants increase, they decrease the supply of oxygen that supports fish, cut off the sunlight, and draw up the water until the lake becomes a swamp. Afterward, depending upon rainfall and other factors, the swamp may become dry land.

That's a natural process, but it's been speeded up in Florida's beautiful lakes. Runoff from highways finds its way into the nearest lake; fertilizer and grass clippings from surrounding lawns add their nutrients to the lake bottom; sewage, raw or treated, may seep in; insecticides and herbicides leach in through the soil; and finally industrial effluents make their debilitating contribution.

Aquatic plants are often beautiful, but beautiful or not, some of these plants are polluting the lakes. The worst offenders are not native flora. Hydrilla, for example, was introduced as an oxygenator for fish bowls and fish ponds. It is today one of the most devastating of weeds that infest the lakes. An established plant may spread at the rate of one foot per day. It's often carried from one lake to another on a boat propeller. It chokes the water both by rooting on the floor and floating on the surface.

Whole lakes have been smothered by water hyacinths. The first water hyacinth supposedly was brought in by a lady who bought it at a Japanese exhibition in 1884. The story is apochryphal, but the results are real. The plant grows so fast that 20 adult hyacinths will cover 20 acres of lake surface in one growing season. The plants often make swimming and boating impossible, and they grow so densely they smother fish. As if that weren't bad enough, when the plants mature and decay, they give off hydrogen sulfide and methane gas.

The Florida Department of Environmental Regulation (DER) has charge of the water supply, and there are regional water districts to recommend and oversee actions. The major method employed to clear up a diseased lake is a draw-down. It's an expensive procedure and a slow one, for it entails diverting the water from the lake for as long as it takes to dry it close to the bottom where the sun can help to purify it.

The real cause of the problems of pollution is, as you have suspected, man. Too many people. Ecologists feel that ideally 50% or, better still, 60% of the land should be left in its natural state. Until the quality of life suffers from overdevelopment, people will flock to a paradise. When it's too badly degraded, it will be too late for nature and man.

With 12 million Floridians and 40 million visitors using the water resources of the state, you don't need any figures to tell you that sewage disposal is a problem. It can no longer be dumped into a river and forgotten. Highly treated waste water is best handled by adding it to spray fields, much as nature cleanses water in the wetlands. However, there aren't enough of these left within reach of the metropolitan areas in which most of the waste water is generated. Experiments by flooding orange groves with refined sewage look promising, but the basic problem is growing, not lessening. If, as at present, 1,000 new residents come to the state every day, then a supply of 123,000 extra gallons of water a day is required to meet their needs, according to a study of consumption made by the University of Florida.

As if the dwindling supply of fresh water, the eutrophication of rivers and lakes, and the treatment of sewage were not major problems enough, the discharge of chemical wastes from agricultural and industrial processings adds a formidable burden to water management. Fish kills are not uncommon, and more and more human illnesses are being traced to pollution in the water supply.

Here and there is a success story. The city of Orlando has set aside a 1,200-acre tract in the northeast corner of Orange County for experimental sewage treatment on man-made wetlands. The land was leveled and 2 million plants and 160,000 tree seedlings were put into the ground. Processed wastewater was carried to the area to be filtered on its way to the aquifer and the tributaries of the St. Johns. It takes forty days for the wetlands to clean the treated water. The system seems to be working well. Fish and the birds that feed on them have returned, and gators are back at home in the sloughs.

Flooding

Flooding is a chronic problem. With much of the land so low, the rainfall so generous, hurricanes such a threat, and the oceans so near, it's small wonder. The levels of the water table and of lakes and rivers rise and fall with the fluctuations in rainfall, with control by dams, and with the amount of water drawn off. Some changes take place over a period of years, some just overnight. Water levels are capricious. They're part of a complex pattern of natural phenomena and must be respected.

Water management districts have contour maps which designate land subject to flooding. There are different degrees of susceptibility to floods: 25, 50, and 100-year floodplains, so called because of the average incidence of major flooding. It's only a rough classification, for no one can predict very far ahead when a flood will occur.

There are varying factors to consider in identifying floodplains. One may be the highest watermark of a lake or river; another may be the highest point to which the sea will rise during a violent storm. Still another may be a low spot seasonally under water, but dry part of the year. Flooding up to watermarks and beyond is likely to come from more than the usual amount of rainfall or from a hurricane. It can even come from a heavy summer storm in an area where drainage is inadequate.

In the first chapter of this book the average rainfalls for cities of each region were given, but the rain doesn't come in even amounts. Two inches could fall during one summer afternoon thundershower. A hurricane could raise the pattern of yearly rainfall, for as much as 45 inches could fall in a few days.

People are tempted to build their homes on the shores of lakes, rivers, and bays. The view is great. The breezes are refreshing. Florida sunsets are spectacular over water. And it's nice to have your own boat at your own doorstep. But fifty feet beyond the high water mark might not be enough if there is an insufficient rise in ground.

Lake, river, and interior wetland sites are not by any means the only threatened locations. Even more prone to severe damage are homes built on the wetlands and barrier islands along the coasts of Florida. Developers grab as much space as they can to build on, for they can make excellent profits from habitations next to water. Not only the wealthy can afford these "choice" locations, for often mobile home parks and apartment buildings are built on flood plains close to water.

Man courts disaster when he interferes with nature's way with floodplains. A prime example of this is the case of the Kissimmee River, which runs 98 miles from south of Orlando to Lake Okeechobee. It used to overflow its banks as it snaked along its spawn of wetlands. That made it difficult for the ranchers whose cattle pastured on its banks to keep track of their boundaries, as well as the limits of state-owned land. The river rises and falls, and its general tendency has been to fall over the long term. That means the ranches have for years occupied land that is sometimes under water and at one time was completely so.

So from 1963 to 1970 engineers spent $27,400,000 to dredge canals to drain the wetlands. There were two of them: one 38 miles long and one 52. The flooding was controlled, but the whole ecology of South Florida was altered.

Fortunately, because the river is on the main watershed feeding Lake Okeechobee, it is under the jurisdiction of the Department of Natural Resources. In 1984 against the protests of the cattlemen, the banks of the first canal were demolished to allow the river to return to its sinuous pattern. That cost $1,400,000, and the work is still going on.

Another river that has suffered from dredging is the Apalachicola River, which has been classified as an Outstanding Florida Water because of its pristine natural beauty. For 30 years the Army Corps of Engineers has cleared the river to allow barges to carry bulk cargo 107 miles to the estuary of Apalachicola Bay. It costs $8 million a year to dredge this river and its tributaries in Georgia and Alabama, but agricultural interests say it's worth it. Environmentalists say the fish, the oyster beds in the bay, the surrounding woods, and the purity of the water are all at stake. The DER, the nearby counties, and the U.S. Congress all have some voice in deciding the issues.

One tool used by communities trying to protect water resources is to persuade the water management offices to declare the lakes and rivers nearby as "Outstanding Florida Waters." This makes them off-limits to sewage treatment plants and stormwater runoff from agriculture and industry. These designations are given waters of exceptional ecological or recreational significance.

Restrictions on the development of floodplains are increasing. The Suwannee River Resource Planning and Management Committee, established in 1981, is the outgrowth of cooperation among the eleven counties on the river's course. The Wekiva River, feeding from the spring of the same name, runs through woodlands of natural beauty. Heavy pressures from builders wanting to put up luxurious homes on its banks are being strongly resisted. The state government has bought as much of the endangered land as it can with funds from some of its programs.

There are several principal arms of the DNR that buy up endangered lands. Each year they receive nominations from local governments and from conservation groups of critical areas for purchase. They grade these in terms of severity or urgency and purchase as many as they can. These programs are: the Conservation and Recreational Land program (CARL), Save Our Rivers, Save Our Coasts, and Save Our Everglades. Still another ecologically important bill, the Surface Water Improvement and Management Act (SWIM), gives water management districts the money to restore rivers and their banks.

It isn't easy. The state spent five years in court trying to establish its title to endangered lands along the Peace River. As an outcome of the suit, the DNR, late in 1987, began drafting a rule to present to the governor and the cabinet establishing an acceptable method for determining the high-water line. Anything below the line by law belongs to the state.

An act of Congress in 1982 called the Coastal Barriers Resources Act (CoBRA) protects half a million acres of barrier reefs and islands, many of them in Florida, by withholding government subsidies, such as co-payments for highways and FHA loans in the endangered areas.

Hurricanes

Hurricanes have been known a long time. The word itself comes from the Carib deity Huarakan, a figure somewhat comparable to the Norse god Thor. They aren't to be confused with tornadoes, or twisters, which originate on land, and which are more local in character, although "tornado" is sometimes used as a generic term for windstorms. In the Pacific a hurricane is known as a typhoon. Both are defined as cyclones, or circling winds, or whirlwinds, but whatever you call them, they originate over water, cover large areas, are accompanied by heavy rain and incredible winds, and are capable of terrible destruction.

The hurricanes to which Florida is vulnerable originate as tropical depressions, spots of very low barometric pressure usually somewhere in the Atlantic off the African coast. A depressed area sucks water and air into itself from the surrounding high pressure areas, and the wind and water then build up into what is known officially as a tropical storm. A scale measuring the wind power and speed of the storm, called the Beaufort Scale, has been developed. It rates the power and speed on a scale from zero (calm, no wind pressure, wind speed under one mile per hour) to 12. The last two items on the scale show the difference between a tropical storm and a hurricane. The tropical storm generates winds of 64-75 miles per hour and a pressure of 14.0 pounds per square foot; the hurricane reaches speeds exceeding 75 mph, and generates a pressure of 17 or more pounds p.s.f.. (A chart of the Beaufort scale and a definition of applicable meteorological terms can be found in Appendix V.)

A hurricane consists of a core of low atmospheric pressure and gentle winds, called the eye, surrounded by a circular band of intensive winds, heavy rainfall, and electrical charges. It builds up energy from the evaporation and precipitation of sea water and loses energy when it passes over land. It usually follows a path from east to west, then curves, traveling from southwest to northeast.

Meterologists speak of 25-year hurricanes and 100-year hurricanes. They choose these terms to designate the heavy storms that occur once in an average of 25 years and the heaviest storms that come once in a century. Some even speak of 500-year hurricanes, but they would be so devastating, you can be glad odds are against their occurring in your lifetime.

Another way to classify them is in five different categories, according to the strength of the wind and the amount of destruction. Gilbert, the major hurricane of 1988, whose winds gusted at more than 200 mph, exceeded the 156-mph qualification for a category 5 hurricane.

As a hurricane begins to build up, it is first reported by satellite to the weather station of the National Hurricane Center in Miami. Ships at sea and weather planes send information that keeps track of the storm's progress. Its movement, however erratic it may appear, is directed by a high pressure system in the Atlantic which is called the Bermuda-Azores high. This system rotates clockwise and moves at random around an area of the ocean the size of the United States. Think of it as a gigantic whip that drives the hurricane revolving around its rim. The hurricane driven by the high pressure system rotates in the opposite direction from the system, counterclockwise.

If you're altogether confused about the direction it takes by now, you're in the same situation that the weather forecasters are. They can tell you *where* the storm is, but not where it's *headed*. They use special nomenclature to describe some of their findings, beginning with "gale warning," which means winds of up to 55 mph. The descriptive terms are found in Appendix V. The last of these is a "hurricane warning," which means hurricane conditions are imminent; they're expected within 24 hours or much less. Don't wait. Take precautions. Get to a safe place, whether it be in a well-built house or in a public shelter.

If you live near the coast, follow the advice of the local authorities on whether or not you should leave your home to seek shelter inland. Go if you are advised to leave. Take your family papers and irreplaceable personal property. Moor boats securely or take them out of the water; board or tape windows and keep them closed; clear porches and patios; lower antennas; store drinking water; put ice in freezer chests; locate the charcoal grill, matches, and first aid kit; fill the gas tank; take a change of clothes.

If you don't have to evacuate, besides securing your windows and loose furnishings, lay in a supply of nonperishable foods, candles, radio and flashlight and batteries to operate them. Move your car to high ground. Make sure your flood and disaster insurance is paid.

There is one case when you should slightly open a window during a hurricane. If you're sheltered in your own home, relieve the pressure by opening a window on the opposite side to the one from which the hurricane is blowing. After the eye passes, close that window and open one on the other side.

Two particularly dangerous spots in which to find yourself are in a mobile home or in a boat. Secondary winds can lift or crush a mobile home. If you're in a boat, the marine warning signal for a hurricane is two flags with red grounds and black square centers hung vertically. Get to shore.

The earliest known hurricane in Florida recorded by Europeans was in 1559. They occur with some regularity, at times more than one severe storm in a year, and sometimes two together, one on the heels of the other. The first names of men and women newly assigned each year in alphabetical order are given to tropical storms, and those that develop into hurricanes bear those names.

The season during which hurricanes strike runs from June 15 to November 15, with September being the height of the season. During the 20th century 21 major hurricanes hit the United States. Below are notes from some of them.

In 1926, 100 persons died in Miami Beach when 12-foot waves filled the streets.

In September 1928, the rains alone resulting from a hurricane broke the inadequate dikes on Lake Okeechobee, taking an estimated 2,500 lives and causing more than $50 million in damages.

In 1935 the barometer hit its lowest point to that date in the Western Hemisphere when it dropped to 26.35 inches. Winds of 175 to 200 miles an hour struck the Keys, wiping out entire land masses, destroying 30 miles of railroad bridge, and killing 400 persons.

In 1960 Donna killed 98% of the wildlife and destroyed most of the trees in many areas of the Keys. For 36 hours sustained gale-force winds, gusting at 180 miles per hour pounded the tiny islands, changing their shapes and wiping some of them out.

Gilbert, which struck in September 1988, spared Florida but ravaged the Caribbean islands and the western coasts of the Gulf of Mexico. In the course of its devastating passage, it broke the record for low barometric pressure by causing a drop to 26.13 inches.

Of the ten named storms a season, an average of six reach hurricane strength, but some never hit land. Meterologists predicted a 43% chance of two severe hurricanes in the 80s. The probabilities of a hurricane's striking any of ten of Florida's major cities in a given year are these:

Miami, Key West	14%
Pensacola, Palm Beach	10
Fort Myers, Apalachicola	7
Tampa, Melbourne/Vero Beach	5
Daytona Beach	2.5
Jacksonville	2

Throughout the six-month hurricane season, Floridians are constantly reminded of safety precautions. Phone books, grocery bags, newspapers, television programs, advertising brochures—all these carry hurricane information and tracking charts. If you haven't reacted to such exposure when a real threat arises, you will certainly be reminded by the bullhorns on police cars as the warning is carried through the streets of towns.

Evacuation procedures have been worked out for all areas where the threats are greatest, but there are problems in putting them into effect. Behavioral studies show that 95% of a population advised to evacuate, will. The first problem will be a huge traffic jam. After that, these are the next problems as one of the central Florida planning councils sees them:

(1) finding housing for refugees in malls, churches, schools
(2) dealing with flooding throughout the refuge city
(3) devastation of mobile homes
(4) electrical blackouts and damage to utilities
(5) inadequate insurance by the refugees.

Rivers will rise an estimated six to eight feet; many lakeside homes will be inundated; sewer systems will not be able to handle wastes and runoff, causing a health hazard; winds will exceed 50 miles an hour during the storm; hospitals will be out of action; drinking water and food will be in short supply; whole counties will be under water.

This is a disaster that *will* happen, but no one knows *when*.

Tornadoes

There are also wind storms that don't give enough warning for evacuation. A tornado is a spinning wind that develops within a thunderstorm or hurricane from the collision of warm lower air with cold upper air. Convection is the culprit again. As the wind begins to spin, the air pressure at its center drops. This low pressure sucks up debris from the ground and forms what an observer sees as a funnel. Usually tornadoes travel from southwest to northeast.

They vary widely in severity. The path of destruction depends on the width of the funnel and the length of time it's in contact with the ground before it wears itself out. It's not the speed with which the winds move (20 to 30 mph), but the torsion that lifts trucks, uproots trees and mobile homes, and flattens buildings.

Per square mile of area, Florida is the second most tornado-prone of the states. Oklahoma has the uncoveted championship with an average of 23.7 occurrences annually per 1,000 square miles; Florida has 21.9, and Indiana 18.0. Over a period of 12 years the state recorded between 59 and 71 tornadoes a year.

Thunderstorms

With the right odds you can escape a hurricane and a tornado, but you're sure to experience the dangers of a thunderstorm. Central Florida is the thunderstorm capital of the United States, with over 80 a year in some areas. They are ubiquitous in summer, often accompanied by strong winds. Although most of them last only a hour or two, they can make up for brevity with intensity. Blinding rain and sometimes hail can make wise travelers pull their cars to the safety of a parking lot or underpass to wait out a storm.

Lightning is an ever-present danger in these storms. In 1981, 110 fatalities were blamed on lightning in Florida, twice the number from any other state. The *Orlando Sentinel* reported that lightning kills more Central Floridians each year than are killed by hurricanes and tornadoes combined.

Sinkholes

If the wind and the rain aren't enough threat, imagine the earth falling away beneath your feet. The bottom has been falling out of spots of Florida for millions of years. The technical name is also the common one: sinkholes. There is an average of 200 of them in a year.

The greatest incidence of sinkholes is in central Florida. They're said to be caused by sand, gravity, weather, and man. Most of them occur during April and May, when the water table may be at its lowest. Their incidence increases in the neighborhood of lakes and ponds, which could be ancient sinkholes themselves.

The immediate collapse of the surface is caused by a fault in the limestone under the soil. The limestone caverns and pores are normally water-filled, but during a drought the formations sometimes crack and allow the heavy topsoil to fall in. The limestone is soluble in acid, and it could also dissolve in acid rain or chemical wastes and thus undermine the surface soil. Incorrectly drilled wells, or just too many of them, can cause a drop of water level below ground and trigger a cave-in. Sometimes there are surface warnings such as small depressions or loosening of tree roots, but many times a sinkhole occurs without warning. And if it happens somewhere, chances are that it may happen nearby again.

Red tide

Each year both coasts are afflicted with a phenomenon called the "red tide." The tide is a discoloration born of a microscopic organism called a *Gymnodinium brevis,* but facetiously called by naturalists "Jim Brevis." Jim is a single-celled organism measuring .001 inch, and normally present in a concentration of 1000 per quart of seawater. During seasonal infestations the concentration can grow to 60 million per quart, a concentration that kills fish, poisons mollusks, and irritates humans. If a human consumes a filter-feeding shellfish, like a clam or an oyster, during a red tide, he can suffer serious illness. The red tide killed 100 tons of fish in the Gulf of Mexico in 1974, causing such a stink along the coast that people were advised to wear face masks.

Pollution and Erosion

The Gulf of Mexico in particular has suffered from pollution due to oil drilling in its waters. Recently the Florida coasts were relieved of the imminent threat of further drilling. It may be only a reprieve, however, and even if nearby rigs are banned, pollution from wells anywhere travels on a loop current that enters through the Yucatan Strait and exits through the Florida Straits.

Erosion is eating away at the white beaches. Wave action sucks away 15 million cubic yards of sand each year. Some sand is returned, some lost to the sea. Part of the cause of the loss is the jetties built to preserve the beaches. Bulkheading doesn't help. It destroys the shallows in which marine life spawns and it interferes with normal wave action which replaces sand. And stagnant water behind beachheads breeds mosquitoes.

Not only is a bad idea to fill, but it's just as bad to dredge. Channels are often cut into subdivisions or mobile home parks near a lake to give everybody access to the water. Often a so-called "waterfront" home is situated on such a body of mostly stagnant water, sharing it with mosquitoes and ground water pollution.

Fish kills happen because of red tide, but there are many other causes. By now, you can probably list them for yourself: acid rain, pesticides, industrial wastes, untreated sewage, accidental spills, oxygen deprivation, boat propellers, and eutrophication of a lake. Sometimes even a person of good will will unwittingly kill fish just by using insecticides. Birds are poisoned that way, too. The ecosystem is in delicate balance.

Heat and sun

At least there is one threat you have personal control over: exposure to the sun. While summer lifestyle in Florida takes you from your air-conditioned home into your air-conditioned car to your air-conditioned destination, you didn't come to the state for this. You won't find much shade under a palm tree, so make your own shade. Wear a broad-brimmed hat or use an umbrella when you go to the beach or pool or out on a lake. Or seek out the comfort of one of the *billion* trees the state plants every ten years. Use sun-blocking agents and wear sunglasses. Overexposure causes skin cancers, and there is also a higher incidence of cataracts from strong light levels.

The humidity won't help emphysema sufferers nor those who have respiratory allergies. Fungus infections also flourish in the moist heat.

On the other hand, the warmth will soothe your rheumatic joints. You won't get a heart attack while shoveling snow. And all that sunshine will lift your spirits. On a winter day when the temperature climbs to 80 degrees, you're encouraged to enjoy reading the weather reports from the rest of the country.

The Florida Almanac lists some temperature readings of interest. The record high for the state was 109 degrees (1931) in Monticello, and the record low -2 (1897) in Tallahassee. The average mean temperatures from north to south are 68.8 and 72.3.

Although the gentle winds that cross the flat land remove some irritants from the air, there are still pockets of pollution near the most congested areas of the state. Measurements of the incidence of ozone reflect the amount of harmful exhaust from fossil fuels, including that from cars. Ozone is considered to be a hazard if .12 parts per million are measured just a single day of the year. The Environmental Protection Agency withholds federal funds from those districts in which it finds poor air quality.

As for allergens, they are seasonal. The air pollution index is published in most daily papers and broadcast on the weather channels of the television stations. Below is the scale used on the basis of parts per million:

0–50	good
51–100	moderate
100–199	unhealthful
200–299	very unhealthful
300 and above	hazardous

Environmental groups

Concerned residents will be welcomed by organized environmental protection groups, both as volunteers and as contributors. A few of the more active organizations are: the Sierra Club, the National Audubon Society, the Wilderness Society, the National Parks and Conservation Association, the Defenders of Wildlife, Greenpeace, the National Wildlife Federation, the Florida League of Conservation Voters, Friends of the Earth, and the Izaak Walton League.

Municipalities have developed growth plans and have included environmental representatives on development and zoning boards. The legislature has responded with funds for the statewide programs. The "green voters" are active at the polls.

Ex-governor, now U.S. Senator Bob Graham, and the present governor, Bob Martinez, both provided leadership in protecting the environment.

After all the bad publicity given to the water hyacinth for fouling the lakes, its propensity for drawing away nutrients has been put to good use. Experimental use of the plants as a filtering device to strip nutrients from wastewater has proven successful. Whether it's commercially viable isn't certain.

A celebration by environmentalists greeted the most recent deauthorization of the cross-Florida Canal by Congress. It has a long history. Actually, there were two canals proposed, only one of which has been completed. In 1909 the first of these was begun in South Florida. It started with the Caloosahatchee River near Fort Myers, then extended through Lake Okeechobee, and finally joined the St. Lucie Canal, emerging near Stuart. You can still buy a ticket for a boat ride through this system.

The second canal was begun during the Depression of the early 1930s as a make-work project with a purpose. It was to begin at Yankeetown in north central Florida on the Withlacoochee River. A canal was then to be cut through the limestone backbone of Florida to the Oklawaha River, which flows into the St. Johns and thence into the Atlantic Ocean.

Both projects were supposed to provide inland waterways for commerce and pleasure. The first one cut through the natural ecosystem of South Florida, and the second one was abandoned when it was realized that a sea-level ship canal joining the Gulf of Mexico and the Atlantic Ocean likely would contaminate the Floridan Aquifer. Nevertheless, the cut made into the highly porous Ocala limestone formation damaged more than nature has been able to repair since.

Then in 1971 only the clamor of environmentalists forestalled the revival of the project as a "barge canal" with locks planned to keep out sea water. One-third of the distance overland to the St. Johns had been finished.

Conservation battles are never completely won. In October 1982 at the request of the U.S. House of Representatives' Committee on Appropriations, the Army Corps of Engineers was directed to update and expand its 1977 economic analysis of the feasibility of the cross-Florida barge canal. In 1977 the Corps had recommended terminating work on the canal, saying adverse environmental concerns were not severe enough, but economic justification for building the canal was marginal.

In the late 80s the idea rose again like the phoenix, and only hard work by two of Florida's representatives put it to rest for the time being. Credit goes to Congressmen Kenneth "Buddy" MacKay of Ocala and Clay Shaw of Fort Lauderdale.

The St. Johns River is the longest of the rivers wholly in Florida. In recent times its headwaters were channeled and drained so that homes and recreation areas could be built on the floodplains. The piping and ditching drained the rainwater into the nearest river system emptying into the Atlantic, leaving the area ripe for subdivisions and parking lots. Besides that, the portion of the river flowing through Jacksonville was no longer fit for bathing or fishing because of urban wastes.

Both these problems have been attacked vigorously. The St. Johns River Water Management District has won the right to levy taxes to buy up to 100,000 acres of flood plain to restore some of the upper reaches of the river to their natural contours. The city also went to work to clean up the river at its doorstep. The results have been very gratifying.

But nature is finicky. At one point, to help cleanse the river and to avoid flooding homes built on the banks, the gates on holding dams were opened too suddenly and completely. Oxygen bubbled out of the churning water, and hundreds of fish suffocated. Water managers learned quickly to regulate the gates to produce a steady flow of smooth water.

Some of the worst environmental pollution is done by unconscionable dumping of industrial wastes. Pesticides such as EDB, Temik, Toxaphene, and Ferriamicide were used to control pests that attack citrus crops, insects that cause scabies in livestock, and fire ants. Not only have such destructive chemicals been dumped into lakes and rivers, but they've also been buried in the ground, where they can find their way into the aquifer.

The U.S. Environmental Protection Agency controls a Superfund to clean up after companies that have caused contamination and cannot get rid of it. One of the worst of these is at the Tower Chemical Company four miles east of Clermont. After the Agency had spent millions to neutralize and burn off the dangerous wastes, they dug up the tarmac and concrete to find buried even worse contaminating material than they had already disposed of.

It looks as though the projected bullet train to join Tampa to Orlando and Miami will be built in the next few years, for the legislature came through with funding. Environmentalists fear it will cut through sensitive lands, such as the Green Swamp, but the legislature is considering it, and designing and financing plans are being made.

Finally, probably because the problem can no longer be brushed under the landfill rug, communities are beginning trash separation programs, which ask for paper, metals, and other recyclable materials to be placed in different containers for collection by the sanitation trucks. It's one program that not only saves some of the environment, but also generates the money to pay for its implementation. The state legislature passed a watered-down recycling bill, setting goals and making counties responsible for their enforcement. The materials to be recycled are newspapers, glass, plastic containers, and aluminium cans.

The Everglades

The national park known as the Everglades was dedicated in 1947 by President Harry S. Truman. It covered 1,226,000 acres, and averaged less than nine feet above sea level. It has grown to 1,500,000 acres, and in 1988 Governor Martinez proposed adding 75,000 more to the eastern portion of the park. This sizable area once supplied half the park's water, but canals and levees that were built have interfered with the natural flow of the water. The tract is undeveloped and is swampland, but it's divided into small parcels with thousands of owners. The governor proposes, but it's up to the U.S. Department of the Interior to implement the addition.

To the north of the national park lies Big Cypress Preserve, which serves as a buffer zone. In April of 1988 President Reagan signed a bill to add 146,000 acres to the preserve, bringing the total up to three quarters of a million acres.

The Everglades National Park itself contains only a portion of the wetlands to which it has given its name. It's the southern-most portion, and includes the brackish mangrove forest along the coasts, Florida Bay (the strait between the mainland and the Keys), and many of the Ten Thousand Islands in the bay and along the southwest coast.

There is no other place on Earth like it. It's a complex sub-tropical world of interdependent plant and animal communities set in a "sea" of grass. The first step that powers the ecology is the drainage of water in the rainy season (June to September) from the headwaters of Lake Okeechobee southward to Florida

Walkways in Everglades National Park keep the visitor dry while he goes through the wetlands.

Bay. Since there's only a tiny gradation in elevation between the source of water and the mouth where it's discharged, the flow is steady, but slow. The moving water is in broad rivers called sloughs. Grasses grow in the shallow streams. Airboats part the grasses as they make their way through the water to give validity to the name "sea of grass."

As the flow of water continues, it charges the aquifer with enough fresh water to keep the saltwater of the Gulf of Mexico and the Atlantic Ocean from inundating it. In a severe drought or in case of interference by man, some salt water can enter the aquifer. When the water supply is sufficient again, it will wash it out.

At the eastern edge of the Everglades is a coastal section known as the pine rocklands, upon which Miami and Homestead are built. On an extension of this formation into the grass and water, the National Park Service has built a 39-mile-long road giving access to the interior for visitors. Several overlooks and trails lead off from the road so that visitors can get a closer look at the teeming life within the 'glades.

The sea of grass is dotted with "islands" of trees. There are hammocks (raised portions) and depressions which accommodate different kinds of plants and animals. The trees, many of which are found nowhere else in the country, have exotic names like gumbo limbo, strangler fig, mastic, poisonwood, and bald cypress. The complex is bordered at the sea by mangrove forests. These tidal-zone trees send out many roots which slow the flow of fresh water. In the brackish water among their roots, small fry and invertebrates find protected pools until they grow large enough to live in the salinity of the sea. A few raised areas among the swamps are designated "coastal prairies."

Any man-made canals or structures, such as the once-proposed Everglades Jetport, interfere with the flow of water in this setting where the ecology is fragile, and where they may threaten the whole system and the animals it supports. Many of these birds and animals are already threatened or endangered species: Florida panther, bald eagle, brown pelican, wood stork, roseate spoonbill, Everglades kite, black bear, indigo snake, and various sea turtles.

So closely are these plants and animals adapted to their peculiar environments that any changes in conditions are reflected in whole groups that share a common system. For example, the alligator hole is found in the center of a ring of willow trees or some other suitable plant growth. For its own comfort the alligator enlarges the hole until it has a nice place to move around under water. During the dry season amphibians and fish take refuge in the pool until the land is again flooded. Another example of a balanced system is the trees that can withstand drought and those that cannot. Those that can, move to edge out the water-loving trees in the long dry spells. But in turn they're contained by fires set by lightning.

In the everglades not part of the park there have been some intrusions on the pattern set by nature. Close to the borders are signs advertising airboat rides through the sea of grass. The constant forays of these noisy boats through the sensitive land destroys the grasses and frightens or harms the wildlife. The thick, fertile muck has been drained to grow crops. Unfortunately, such land cannot be returned to its natural state nor replenished. Reclaimed farmland would no longer be covered with saw grass, but with a mixture of native trees and exotics that would change the natural balance. Once the blanket of water has been channeled away and the soil plowed, the land is no longer able to support its unique ecosystem. Areas still salvageable on the margin of the park are those sought by Governor Martinez.

If you follow the road from Florida City through the national park, you will come to the edge of Florida Bay. There you will find a welcome center, a restaurant, a marina, a motel, and a campground. Boat rides are available and canoes may be hired. Still another access road to the park leads off the Tamiami Trail (U.S. 41). Tram tours are the best way to see this area. At the end of the ride is an observation tower. If you move to Florida, try seeing the park during the late fall before the heavy influx of tourists. At any time of year, whatever else you bring, don't forget the insect repellent. Mosquitoes have their world headquarters in the everglades.

If you cannot go in person, or if you want to prepare for your visit, you can do no better than to read the moving classic by Marjory Stoneman Douglas, *The Everglades: River of Grass*. A new edition was printed in 1988 on the occasion of the author's 98th year of life. A listing is in the bibliography.

A sixfold plan was begun during the administration of Governor Bob Graham under the aegis of Save Our Everglades. If and when it's fully implemented, it will affect the flow of water from the Kissimmee River to Florida Bay particularly, and the natural water cycle of the state generally. The idea is that by the year 2000, the natural systems in South Florida will again operate much as they did in the year 1900.

The first item on the plan is the restoration of the wetlands by freeing the Kissimmee River, as explained earlier. Next, state-owned lands elsewhere will be swapped for privately-held land south of Lake Okeechobee. Third, dams and culverts will be redesigned or eliminated in a wide area north of the national park, including facilitation of water flow under Alligator Alley and the Tamiami Trail. The fourth part is the purchase of lands in the eastern Everglades to add to the park. The fifth and sixth projects are concerned with wildlife management, including protection for the habitats of the Everglades deer and the Florida panther.

Man isn't alone in this subtropical world. There are familiar and exotic plants. There are birds and insects, land animals and aquatic creatures. Maple trees like those "back home" grow next to tall, slender royal palms; mockingbirds share the airways with egrets; armadillos and raccoons run on the forest floors; and alligators that never saw a Northern lake, swim smoothly along the warm waters.

11. Growing Things

The chapter you're about to read can't begin to cover the botanical specimens of Florida. There are many excellent books about growing things, some of which are mentioned in the bibliography, and others which may be purchased, or borrowed at a library. However, the following few pages make some general statements, examine a few interesting specimens, and pass along some suggestions that can be helpful to a new resident.

Generally speaking, you'll need to fertilize more often, water less, and fight different insects in Florida than you did back home. The rains fall in the summer when your garden needs them most. However, the humidity is also high, encouraging the growth of fungi. You'll need to sprinkle the leaves of ornamentals with sulfur products to discourage mold. The nutrients leach freely from the sandy soil, so if you use compost instead of chemical fertilizers, you'll have more lasting results. As for the insects, natural controls are best. There are some tips in this chapter, and in the next under the subhead "Insects."

A reminder is in order before you put spade to earth. Make sure there are no underground pipes or connections where you plan to dig. They're not buried very deeply in Florida soil.

Palm trees

Palm trees have a great appeal to new Floridians, and planting at least one of them asserts the acceptance and pride of the neophyte with this indisputable badge of the tropics. They're very easy to care for. They're hardy for most Florida localities, don't require much fertilizer, and have few natural enemies. Once in a while you might want to cut away the old leaves that turn brown or the seed spathes that keep sprouting. Otherwise, you can treat them with benign neglect.

There are more than 40 kinds of palm trees in the state, 15 of which are native. Basically they have two types of leaves: the palmate, which spread out from a single center like a fan or the fingers on your hand; and the pinnate, that grow along a stem like feathers or the teeth of a comb. You might like to note that palm trees have their roots in a clump, not spread out like those

Salt-tolerant plants on a Gulf beach—sea grapes and succulents beyond the tide line.

of a "proper" tree. Don't be upset if the specimen you buy looks almost rootless.

Palm trees are often grouped close together or are arranged in rows. You might want to plant three of the single-trunked varieties for a better effect.

Here are a few common types to consider:

Sabal palm.   This native is the state tree of Florida and probably the best all-around palm for landscape use. It has a slender trunk with a terminal bud that sprouts leaves that look like a drooping fan. The bud can be served as a vegetable known as hearts of palm, but don't do that if you want to keep the tree. The "vegetable" gives the tree its common name: cabbage palm. As the tree grows, the boots (stubs) of the shed branches make a crisscross pattern along the trunk. After a time the trunk smoothes and crisscrossing stubs show only at the top of the tree.

Plumosa.   This is probably the second most common palm tree. It can grow to 50 feet and is smooth of trunk. It can be raised easily from a seed, and its growth is rapid. The leaves are feathery and form great arching plumes. While it is generally hardy, some specimens were harmed by the killing frosts that destroyed the orange groves in central Florida.

Royal palm. This is a beauty, but it's too big to plant in most front yards. It's a tree used for lining broad avenues. The trunk is smooth and very slender, and the leaves are palmate. In Palm Beach, Fort Myers, and other cities you'll find them gracing long avenues.

Areca palm.   There are many names for this small palm tree that grows in clumps of five or more. It's also called cane and yellow butterfly and Madagascar palm. It's great for foundation planting because it doesn't crowd other plants, although eventually it will grow tall. Its leaves are pinnate and curved, its trunks slim, and its whole aspect very tropical.

Pindo palm.   This is a short, relatively slow-growing palm with a trunk that may remind you of a pineapple in shape. The

A cluster of sabal palms, Florida's state tree.

leaves are plentiful, coarse, pinnate, and arranged on deeply curving stalks. It doesn't grow very high, but its leaves are spread out so that it needs eight or ten feet of space on all sides. The pineapple effect of the bulbous trunk is heightened by the boots of the old stems that have been removed or died.

Chinese fan palm.   If you want a single tree that spreads out to provide shade, you can try this one. Leave plenty of room, for it grows 20 feet high and can spread to 15 feet in width. The leaves are palmate and grow densely on a substantial trunk.

Flowering trees:

Besides the palms, there are some exotic flowering trees to brighten your life. The jacaranda, while it grows erratically and asymmetrically, has great panicles of blue-violet color that glorify the landscape in April and May. Although it freezes at 26 degrees, it can recover. The golden raintrees put on their brilliant show in the fall. First they show yellow flowers which soon fall in a "golden rain"; then beautiful pink seed pods cover the tree; last these fade to a uniform beige, still beautiful to the eye. A raintree might sprout seedlings all over your yard, which might bother you a bit. But the beautiful tree is worth it, and you can share the seedlings with your neighbors.

The Southern magnolia, another beauty, has big, glossy, evergreen leaves that resemble those of a rhododendron, and white, waxy flowers that bloom in the spring. The flowers are large and showy, but you may have to prune the tree if it seems to be getting too big for your lot. Another white flowering tree with lovely, glossy leaves has the alliterative name of loblolly bay.

Fruiting trees

If you prefer food with your landscaping, you might want to try a banana tree. It's classified as herbaceous rather than arboreal, but since it grows as tall as eight feet, it's very treelike. It grows quickly and bears the second year. The fruit, commonly called "lady fingers," is a small banana with a thin yellow skin. Like regular bananas, the fruit grows on a single spike.

The trunk is not woody, but composed of layers; the leaves are pale green, broad and flat. The tree will answer your wish for something exotic and tropical to look at, even if it doesn't bear every season. Put it in a protected spot, for it's very tender.

If you live in the southern third of the peninsula, you can combine shade and fruit by planting a mango tree. The trees are tender and can be damaged by temperatures of 26 degrees. They can grow very tall, so if you can buy a dwarf variety, it would be a good idea. The fruit is sweet to eat from your hand like a peach, but it also makes good pies and flavors ice cream. A few people can't eat mangos without developing a rash.

The avocado tree is just as accommodating with its shade, and will grow only half as tall. Furthermore, it's an evergreen and reasonably hardy. You'll have more fruit than you can eat in salads and dips.

Papayas are easier to harvest, for they grow on herbaceous stems rather than trunks. They blossom three or four months after sprouting. The fruit grows in clusters at the top of the stem. It's usually eaten like a melon with a spoon. Papain, the food product used for tenderizing, is found in the sap. The plants are susceptible to damage at 30 degrees or less but can be replaced more easily than a tree.

Citrus

Among fruit trees, citrus is king. Besides grapefruit and oranges, you can grow limes, tangerines, lemons, and hybrids such as tangelos. Furthermore, citrus requires little fertilizer and doesn't like its feet wet. Oranges grown in the sandy soil of Florida are great for juice. While oranges grown in California's drier climate are easier to peel and eat out of hand, there are also navel oranges in Florida that natives say are superior. The lemons you grow won't look the same as the California variety that are commonly sold, but the flavor is excellent.

Don't try to grow a tree from a seed. You might get good fruit, and you might not. The trees in the groves are all prepared by grafting budstock from trees with known characteristics onto rootstock that will support them. Go to a nurseryman and ask his advice as to the best kind and his guidance in growing your citrus. Here is some information to help you make a choice:

> Navel orange, season from November to January—
>   peel it and eat it from your hand;
> Hamlin orange, October to December—great for
>   squeezing;
> Pineapple orange, December to February—sweet,
>   fragrant juice orange;
> Valencia orange, March to July: This versatile
>   orange accounts for half the juice crop;
> Temple orange, January to March—seedy, reddish-
>   orange spicy fruit for eating;
> Murcott hybrid, January to March—tasty cross
>   between an orange and a tangerine;
> Minneola hybrid, January—cross between a
>   tangerine and a grapefruit;

Marsh grapefruit, November to June—yellow,
   almost seedless, sections easily, sweet taste;
Pink seedless grapefruit, October to May—like the
   Marsh, except for color;
Duncan grapefruit, October to May—large yellow
   fruit, with many seeds, but great flavor and juice;
Dancy tangerine, December to January—large crops
   of small fruit.

Shade trees

It's going to be hot in the summer in your Florida home, and nature has thoughtfully provided its own air conditioning. You're lucky if someone has planted a shade tree some time ago for your use, but if not, you can plant one for yourself and the next person. A native called the live oak is monarch among trees of the Southeast United States. It doesn't grow fast, but it lasts forever. This accommodating tree spreads its branches wider than it grows tall. The leaves are small, dark green above and pale and hairy below, but they grow in such quantity, the shade they generate is dense, and although the tree drops its leaves once a year, it immediately replaces them. They don't look at all like the leaves of the oak trees common in the North, but they do bear small acorns to show their relationship.

The turkey oak doesn't get as tall nor live so long as the live oak, but it thrives in poor soil. In the fall it makes a show of brilliant color before dropping its leaves.

The average drake elm grows no higher than 25 feet, keeping it within bounds for a small lot. Although it's deciduous, its leaves regrow in a matter of ten weeks.

The sweetgum, sycamore, locust, tulip, and maple can follow you down South, where they will grow well and quickly. They lose their leaves for about three months of the year and even give a subdued show of color in the fall. Many tree seedlings are distributed free or sold at nominal prices when released by the state Department of Agriculture.

Several varieties of pines are native to Florida and make excellent perimeter plantings. The long leaf pine is a beauty, grows rapidly, and offers a good home to birds. They will be symmetrical if you plant each with enough room to grow.

Camphor trees have a wide, spreading pattern of growth and dense shade. Crushed leaves smell of camphor. They're not so common as live oaks, but they have one special advantage: they don't attract Spanish moss.

Spanish moss is an air plant that attaches itself to tree branches and even to wires. Its nourishment comes from sunshine and from the water it absorbs from the air. It looks like gray beards hanging from whatever supports it finds. It has some uses: commercially it was harvested for stuffing and packing materials; birds use it for building nests. But it also can grow so dense it can deprive a tree of sunlight and eventually kill it. It's spread by the wind.

The bald cypress is a slow-growing tree with few branches and leaves and a trunk with rough bark and vertical indentations. It's an evergreen related to the pine family, and a favorite settling place for Spanish moss. Cypress trees grow in wetlands or near the shores of lakes. Characteristic knobby growths called knees push up from the underwater roots. There are at least two popular explanations for the functions of these knees: either they're to brace the tree in the wet soil or they're to help the roots "breathe."

As you drive along the highways you'll see cypress clocks, tabletops, and plaques for sale. These are slices of trunks whose unusually deep indentations make each piece individualistic. The slices are highly polished and given some decorative function. Naturalists grieve when they see a hundred years' growth of tree cut up for commercial uses of no special benefit. Cypress trees in lakes are protected, but some are on private land so they can be harvested.

Maverick trees. Three trees to avoid planting are the Brazilian pepper, the cajeput or punk tree, and the Australian pine. All are examples of imports brought to Florida for good enough reasons, but which have now gone wild to an alarming extent, taking over the territory of valuable native plants. Once you can

Moss-draped bald cypress trees.

recognize these three, you'll realize just how much of Florida they cover. The Brazilian pepper is a large shrub with red berries in winter. The cajeput is a papery-barked tree with white flowers off and on during the year, and with pollen that is irritating to many. The Australian pine looks like a pine, but isn't, can grow quite tall, and is found along many beaches. A number of Florida cities have outlawed any further planting of these fast-growing pests, and some communities have even provided for their removal.

Shrubs and decorative trees

For landscaping purposes quick growing shrubs and decorative trees are excellent choices. The Norfolk Island pine is a good example. It has dark green stiff branches growing in horizontal circles in perfect symmetry. The crape myrtle is a bush that grows red, pink, mauve, or white blooms in clusters in July. Two other attractive and easy to recognize candidates are the bottle brush tree and the powderpuff tree. The dogwood, probably an old friend from back home, does well in Florida, too.

Red, pink, white, or yellow oleanders are large bushes with stiff, pointed leaves and clusters of blooms. They're often grown on median strips or along the shoulders of highways. All parts of these beautiful plants are poisonous, however. Animals have died from eating the leaves, and even the smell of burning oleander wood is toxic.

You'll see many Spanish bayonets in home plantings. These have narrow trunks, which sometimes grow in a sinuous pattern, and sharp, pointed leaves that stick out like swords from the tops of the trunks. The gentler schefflera is spectacular if grown in a protected spot outdoors. Although it freezes at 29 degrees, it will grow back. It's sometimes called an umbrella tree because each set of broad leaves is like a shiny green open umbrella. It grows well indoors, and it comes in a dwarf variety.

Also great indoors is that favorite of shopping malls, the fig. You can get a nice effect by trimming off lower branches, and as the upper ones spread out too far for your indoor space, you can prune them back. A third indoor small tree/shrub is the massangeana cane, commonly called the corn plant. It does have long, broad, coarse leaves that resemble those on a corn stalk, but they grow from a straight woody trunk, and look somewhat like a small palm tree. They tolerate low light conditions. Nurserymen have them, but they're so common, you can probably buy one at the local supermarket.

Bamboo is showy if you have enough room for it and want to make a screen at the edge of your property. It has the familiar canes topped with feathery leaves. But it grows fast and dense, and spreads quickly. You'll need a lot of room. Yet another nice shrub that's showy in the summer is pampas grass. It sends up stems eight feet tall, whose feathery leaves can be sprayed with a lacquer, brought indoors, and put in tall vases. Check them for mites first.

You might like to grow a cactus called the prickly pear. It flowers and bears edible fruit, but the plants have very sharp spines. Camellias come dressed in red, white, pink, or variegated blooms that look as though they should smell heavenly, but don't. The leaves are glossy, the bush shapely, and only the flowers that turn brown as they die detract from their beauty. In that respect they're like the azaleas with which you're probably familiar. Azaleas bloom twice a year in Florida. Just keep the soil acid and sprinkle for fungus.

Gardenias outdoors in the warm climate are a sight to behold. If you feed and protect one with the same care recommended for the azalea, you can grow a plant eight feet tall which is covered with hundreds of fragrant white blooms twice a year. It may succumb to frost, but it will revive. Hibiscus also loses its leaves and tender wood in a freeze, but when it's cut back, it will be beautiful again the next spring. The lilylike blooms are single or double in red, orange, yellow, pink, white, and mottled colors.

An oddity is the century plant. A big rosette of spikes and a "trunk" left when the spikes fall off characterize this succulent plant. The leaves look something like those on the familiar houseplant known variously as a snake plant, Indian feather, or sansevieria. You could grow a row of them for a thick fence. They like sun and don't mind salt. But once in ten years, a 30-foot spike will climb skyward out of the top of the parent plant, bear its seeds on its shaky top, and drop them as the old plant dies.

Fruiting plants

Near the sea or inland you can grow the salt-tolerant treelike shrub called the sea grape. It has distinctive round leaves up to eight inches across, small white flowers that grow in long clusters, and grapelike fruit that is too tart to eat, but makes excellent jelly and wine. The native sea grape will adapt itself to espaliers.

Another bush whose fruit you'll enjoy is the blueberry. If you have room to plant a row of one of the species recommended, you'll be able to harvest them between March and May, months before they ripen back home. Raspberries aren't available yet, but the agricultural experts are working on them.

It's possible for you to pick strawberries out of your yard for Christmas dinner if you plant them in early fall. Commercially, however, they're harvested between February and April. You can save yourself the trouble of growing blueberries and strawberries if you wait until the growers open their fields at the end of the season. Then you can bring containers and pick as much as you can eat and freeze or can for bargain prices.

Flowers and foundation plants

Many of the annuals you grew up North will flourish in Florida, and you can plant them twice a year—in October and February, or whenever they appear in the nurseries. The sandy, quick-draining soil won't work as well as loams do, but there's a special trick that produces excellent results. Plant your seed or starter plants in pots of prepared soil and sink them into the ground. Then cover them with mulch. Not only will they be protected from competition with other plants that way, but some measure of protection from root-eating pests will be provided.

Another neat way to grow annuals and related plants is to put them in hanging baskets. They look festive and can always be moved to a protected spot in case of excessive wind or frost. Impatiens and petunias like this treatment. Fuchsias look spectacular hanging their lady's eardrops from their drooping stems.

Among the most popular of the perennials are the chrysanthemums. They naturally bloom in the fall, but by controlling light, you can force them to bloom at almost any time. Bulbs that brighten the spring will also flower at any season provided you keep them in the refrigerator for eight to twelve weeks to allow them the dormant period provided by cold weather.

If you want color, try some of these suggestions. Kalanchoes in warm reds and oranges make excellent bedding plants. Geraniums love sun and will grow well in the cooler Florida months. Crotons, with their colorful foliage, make a splash if you don't let them get too cold. The oyster plant has purple-green knifelike leaves and is easy to grow. Caladiums, elephant ears, and begonias also dress up ordinary greens with unexpected colors. Variegated holly adds silver to its pale green foliage. And if you plant some of the many-hued day lilies, they'll brighten your May garden.

Your rose garden will bloom around the year if you allow for brief vacations when it's too hot or too cold for the plants. After a bush has bloomed, cut it back drastically or it will grow spindly and out of shape. An old enemy, black spot, likes to infest rose leaves, but will succumb to sulfur dusting. At least there will be no early summer infestation of Japanese beetles to feast on your lovely flowers.

Boston ferns like the climate. You can even make them grow up the stubs of old palm leaves on a pindo palm. There's no shortage of green plants, for Florida has two cities famous for their foliage: Apopka and Lake Placid.

Aloe vera has an interesting shape with its long, pointed, green fingers. It's a plant highly touted for its emollient juices that are used in sun tan oils and face creams. You can easily extract the juice by cutting off a "leaf" and peeling it. Some people drink the juice, which is processed, and sold in health food stores. But one of the most common applications of aloe vera is the treatment of burns. Just rub the raw juice on the burn. Serious burns, of course, require professional treatment. Even though it's good for treating burns, the plant doesn't like long exposure to direct sunlight. The mother plant is usually surrounded with young shoots, and if you break one off, you can easily grow another from it.

Jasmine and bougainvillea sprawl in a manner that makes them excellent for use as vines or on a trellis or espalier. Both come in several varieties. Bougainvillea hangs its cascade of purple, red, or orange over fences, walls, or balconies. Jasmine has glossy leaves, and many varieties are fragrant. There's a popular flame vine, too, with matchstick red tubular blooms.

Indoor gardening in Florida rooms permits the growth of tender plants that are truly tropical. Anthuriums grow a long tongue thrusting out from a curved sheath. Birds-of-paradise point flying red fingers. Gloxinias glow with particolored blooms. The succulents known as Christmas cactus bloom at least twice a year. You can break off a couple of sections of the leaves and stick one end in soil to propagate new plants; this is especially useful when the mother plants become too large. Watering once a week is sufficient.

Many epiphytes need the protection of indoors. They're plants that get their nourishment and water from the air, but attach themselves to other media for a foothold. Among the flowering varieties are orchids and bromeliads. Orchids need filtered light in summer and a sunny window in winter, for they don't like direct sunlight or the cold. There's one variety with green-yellow flowers called *Vanilla fragrans* that produces home-grown vanilla beans. Orchids are available and enticing, but they're not very easy to grow.

A nonflowering epiphyte with the descriptive name of staghorn is popular with Floridians. It can be fastened to posts or walls or trees or it can hang in a basket with some sphagnum moss to anchor it. The basket is probably the best way to grow it because it, too, is susceptible to frost and direct sunlight.

Poinsettias grow and grow until they're taller than most persons if they're in a protected location and have good weather. The usual practice is to prune them down to keep them from getting spindly. If you buy a plant at Christmastime, its brachts will still be red in April. Put it outdoors when the frost is over. At first it will look sick, but it will perk up later and begin to grow. It has one finicky characteristic: it won't bloom if it doesn't get a certain number of hours of darkness for a month or more before its time. Be sure it isn't located where an artificial light will frustrate its natural order.

A last word about plants needs mention. Besides the oleander, there are others that are classified as poisonous. The poinsettia, elephant ear, century plant, oyster plant, and even the bulbs of daffodil, hyacinth, and narcissus can be harmful. That's not a complete list of poisonous plants, of course. For a good listing and description of Florida's poisonous plants, see George Campbell's book, listed in the bibliography.

Garden foods

Vegetables are planted at different times in the three temperature bands of Florida. Planting times are earlier than you might be used to, and often you can raise several crops in a year. In the central band, planting begins early in March and extends through April. It's well to plant small amounts a week apart to insure a continuing supply rather than a glut at a single harvest.

The most popular vegetables are green beans, beets, members of the cabbage family, carrots, celery, corn, cucumbers, eggplant, escarole, herbs, leeks, lettuce, okra, onions, peas, peppers, potatoes, pumpkins, radishes, spinach, squash and tomatoes.

Besides blueberries and strawberries, melons are popular garden fruits, but you can also grow peaches, pears, plums, pecans, and citrus if you don't mind waiting for a few years until the trees bear. Dwarf trees are recommended, both because they have smaller crops and they're easier to pick. Hardware and garden stores sell a wire basket to attach to a wooden handle for harvesting hard-to-reach citrus fruits.

Ground covers

Besides aggregates and mulches that can be used effectively instead of grass, there are many growing plants that make excellent ground covers. The local nursery can be helpful in recommending these, but herewith are a few you might consider.

The most popular is wedelia, which likes sun. Boston ferns and asparagus ferns, although they're often used in hanging plants, likewise fill in quickly; they prefer shade, but can withstand sun. Periwinkle, also known as vinca, is a good choice and as a bonus has seasonal blooms. Juniper takes a while to get started, but makes a thick, low blanket that's frostproof. A few others you might look at are blood leaf, dwarf lantana, and holly-leaf malpighia.

Lawn grasses

The grass on your Florida lawn will be coarse. It can be planted by flats of sod, plugs, sprigs, or seeds, and will grow most effectively in that order. You can also grow fine ryegrass from seeds for quick cover, but it doesn't make a permanent lawn.

Three varieties are most often planted: Bahia, St. Augustine, and Seville. The Bahia has finer blades, but is less durable, and it's the first choice of a pest called the mole cricket. St. Augustine is coarser and more amenable to bad conditions; it is also the favorite food of a critter, the chinch bug. Seville is as coarse, but hardier and denser than the other two. So far no special insect has stated its preference for Seville, which doesn't mean it's not infested.

All three of these grasses send out runners, called stolons, to start up new plants, like zoysia, with which you may be familiar. The stolons allow it to spread quickly, but they're often intrusive in flower beds.

Seville is gaining in popularity. It's sold in trays of individual plugs, and the nursery at which you buy it will lend or rent a plugger to you. It can be planted without too much trouble that way. For quick spreading it can be inserted in cleared soil, but it will also take over other grasses or weeds if plugs are spaced in existing lawns. It needs frequent watering for a good start.

Nonpolluting treatments

There are three main groups of pesticides according to what they're composed of. These are: inorganic, organic, and synthetic. The inorganic pesticides are made from minerals, such as sulfur and copper. Organics are made from plants, as in pyrethrins and nicotine. Synthetics are carbohydrates to which chemicals have been added, as in malathion. A fourth type of control is made of organisms developed in a laboratory, such as bacteria that can invade a pest.

All types disturb the environment to some extent. They injure plants and living creatures, they harm the soil, and they seep into the water supply. They're spread by wind and air, runoff, leaching, and by getting into the food chain. Of them all, however, the organics are least harmful. They include rotenone, pyrethrum, sabadilla, and ryanis that are sold in garden shops. The first two are toxic, and must be used with care.

Among the methods for control without pesticides are planting varieties of plants and seeds that are resistant to pests. It's

also possible to plant repellents, such as marigolds, among vegetables. Third, it's useful to introduce biological controls:
insect-eating birds, parasites, and preying insects. You can even
order ladybugs by mail. Fourth, sanitary practices in planting
and in removing debris where critters can thrive are helpful.

Besides these, you can resort to physical methods with traps,
heat and cold, and screens. Light is another means of control:
blue light attracts bugs to the electric zappers, and yellow light
keeps them away from your patio and doorstep. Except that tiny
white flies are attracted to a board painted yellow on which you
have spread something sticky and sweet to trap them. Beetles
will drown in a shallow bowl of flat beer.

The following is a partial list of birds that nest in Florida and
that use insects as the major portion of their food: painted bunt-
ing, summer tanager, parula warbler, Eastern meadowlark, yel-
lowthroat, white-eyed vireo, starling, Eastern bluebird,
Carolina and house wrens, scrub jay, purple martin, barn swal-
low, great crested flycatcher, Eastern kingbird, downy wood-
pecker, yellow shafted-flicker, and kildeer. To test the likelihood
of a bird's preferring insects to grain or berries, put out some
suet. The insectivorous birds will eat it.

If you must use a pesticide, first be certain of the pest you
want to eradicate. Then read the label to determine whether the
product is applicable and the level of its toxicity. The law
requires labeling to use three terms to describe toxicity:

Danger, a teaspoonful or as little as a taste can kill an average
person;

Warning, a tablespoonful or less is lethal;

Caution, one part in sixteen can kill.

It's common for people to feel they aren't susceptible to a poison that is used on such inconsequential things as insects, but
they share the basic building blocks of life with humans. Use
only what poisons you must, and put them on the specific plants
for which they're intended on a day when there's little wind.

Avoid chemical fertilizers when compost will do the job. You
can buy soil with high organic content or make your own from

decaying clippings and leaves and from wastes in food preparation.

There are many creatures that share our world. Some of them in the Sunshine State may need to be introduced to new citizens. Others are old friends. In the next chapter we'll look at a few of particular interest.

12. Living Things

Animals are amazing creatures. For their weight, they're much stronger and have more stamina than humans. A tiny bird can fly thousands of miles in its annual migration. A squirrel can climb a trunk as fast as a car can move on a suburban street. A deer or a preying wild cat can outspeed the fastest sprinter. The acrobatics of monkeys in the treetops are smoother, faster, and more daring than those of a human gymnast.

Still, wild animals are losing their homes and their lives to people every day. Their habitats and their food supply are disappearing as human demands encroach on them. The world is the poorer as each species dies out, and perhaps someday there will be only natural preserves in which they can live. Human needs are paramount, for humans have said so, but caring people among them work to save what they can of animal life to enrich their children's world.

Animals

There are 150 native species of amphibians and reptiles in the state. Many of them are small, like the frog, the salamander, the newt, and the gecko. Some are big like the turtles and tortoises; some are helpful, like the garden snake, and some are poisonous, like the rattler. But, dominating them all is the anachronistic amphibian known as the alligator.

Alligators

The young of alligators hatch from a clutch of 20 to 60 eggs laid in May or June in a nest of vegetation mixed with soil built up by the female. Incubation time is about three months, and in most parts of Florida hatching takes place between August 15 and September 15. The young are tiny yellow and black copies of their all-black elders. They eat mostly insects and small invertebrates as well as small fish, so that by the end of a year they have grown appreciably. In most parts of their range, when feeding conditions are good, an alligator will grow approximately a foot a year until it's about eight feet long. There is some variation, however, as full-grown females average half the size of males. A female may produce her first small nest at six or seven years of age.

The mother alligator guards her nest aggressively before the eggs are hatched. Then she aids the young in their release and carries them in her mouth to the aquatic nursery site she has selected. There she protects them for almost a year until the next breeding season.

Mating time is usually early April and May but varies in warmer parts of the alligator's large range. If you're near an adult population, you can hear both males and females bellow as a means of communication. Sounds produced by alligators vary and can range from a croaking yelp, the juvenile distress call, to a roar, depending on the message being sent.

Alligators have the valuable habit of digging dens or "gator holes," which are simply ponds the alligator maintains with sufficient depth to provide year-round fresh water. The gator hole is deeper than the lowest water table, and during the dry season in some localities, it's the only natural fresh water available. It provides a home not only for the alligator, but also for turtles, fish, and other wildlife. Some of these are food for the gator, but they come to the hole, anyway, for it's their only chance to survive the dry season. Birds are also attracted to the pool for water and food. All are links in that great congregation of nature, the food chain.

Will an alligator attack a man? Ordinarily alligators avoid people, but people who don't leave them alone are in danger. Don't swim where they've been spotted or even suspected. Don't go near females when they're guarding their nests. Don't approach those that are sunning themselves on a bank. Don't leave your pet where it is vulnerable to attack. Don't try to move faster than they do. And don't *ever* feed them. An alligator who is "tamed" by being fed presents the same problem as the bears that are fed by unwise visitors to our national parks. If then left unfed for some reason, the animal becomes potentially danger-ous when it comes to inhabited areas in search of handouts. A fed alligator has lost its fear of man, and its boldness spells dan-ger. The state has underscored the danger by declaring that feed-ing wild alligators is a second-degree misdemeanor, punishable by 60 days in jail or a $500 fine.

Alligators are at home in the water or on land. In water they have to come up eventually for air, but they can stay below the surface for as long as three-quarters of an hour. When the tem-perature drops below the level of comfort for these cold-blooded creatures, they seek out a sunny bank.

To keep the record straight, there are two major differences in appearance between the crocodile and the alligator. The croco-dile has a longer, narrower snout and lighter coloring than its rel-ative. The croc also prefers brackish water to fresh water. Its numbers are few in this country, but a refuge has been estab-lished on Key Largo to protect the species.

The small amphibians and reptiles are insectivorous and should be encouraged to make their homes in your garden. Toads are particularly helpful, and in quiet neighborhoods you can see them at night sitting in lighted areas waiting immobile for some unsuspecting bug.

Snakes

There are many harmless and much-maligned snakes in Florida, just as there are in the rest of the country. Only four species give a bad name to local serpents.

The cottonmouth moccasin, a semi-aquatic snake, gets its name from the white interior of its mouth. It grows as long as four feet with a diameter of three inches, so that it classifies as a big and heavy snake. The moccasin makes its home in fresh water: lakes, swamps, marshes, and ponds. When it isn't swimming about looking for its next meal, it finds an overhanging branch or a floating log on which to sun itself. The young snakes are a cocoa brown with irregular bands of dark brown. As they age, their colors fade to dull olive and black, but they retain yellow streaks on their heads. Their poison is deadly, causing gangrene and tetanus.

The diamondback rattlesnake sometimes grows to eight or nine feet, while the related dusky pygmy rattlesnake grows only to a foot and a half. Rattlesnakes of both sizes make their home in piny and palmetto woods, but may be found in other locales, including beaches. They're olive-colored with dark diamonds outlined in yellow. Rattlesnakes are ill-tempered reptiles, and they don't always make a warning rattle when they get ready to strike. If you're in the woods, step *on* fallen logs, rather than *over* them.

The deadliest of all is the long slender, beautifully colored coral snake. Its size ranges between two and three-and-a-half feet. The snake looks much like another harmless variety, the king snake. Both are banded orange-red and black, but the coral snake has a distinctive black nose, and its slightly different pattern of coloring is described by a little rhyme to help humans differentiate them:

> "Red touch yellow, kill a fellow;
> Red touch black, good for Jack."

If you see red, black, and yellow, don't wait to examine the pattern, for the coral snake's venom paralyzes the lungs and hearts of its victims. They usually hide under rocks or burrow in the ground seeking a cool, dark spot. Fortunately, this snake isn't aggressive unless it's confined or cornered, and due to its small size, its bite must be administered to an exposed and tender area of the skin for envenomation to take place.

Last is the copperhead, who is probably native to your home state. It doesn't like heat, so its territory in Florida is confined to the northern third, particularly the Panhandle.

To protect yourself wear boots in the woods or high grass; keep screen doors closed tight; if you see a snake, let him alone; if you're bitten, call the poison center or a hospital. Remember that snakes are more beneficial than harmful. They keep to themselves most of the time, and they do kill vermin like rats and mice.

Sea turtles

One of the very interesting phenomena that a nature-lover can observe on certain beaches in the state is the ritual of marine turtles coming ashore to lay their eggs. The nesting sites are protected by wildlife officers who control the number of observers and keep their actions from disturbing the turtles. A second observation period occurs at hatching time when the young fight their way out of their eggs and struggle down the beach to the sea. Among the most popular sites for turtle watching are the beaches of Brevard County.

Four major sea turtle species use the coast as their breeding grounds: loggerheads, greens, Kemp's ridley, and leatherbacks. The nesting period runs from May to October, but the usual time to watch the hatching is June and July. To learn the schedule for organized watches, write to the Chambers of Commerce in Melbourne and Jensen Beach. In Melbourne the address is 1005 E Strawbridge Avenue, zip 32901; in Jensen Beach it's 1910 NE Jensen Beach Boulevard, zip 33457.

The loggerhead sea turtle comes ashore to nest on the Atlantic Coast from North Carolina to Florida. The leatherback and green turtles nest on Florida's east coast. Kemp's ridleys are rare, for it's estimated that only 1,000 adults remain worldwide. The females come ashore at night to lay about 120 round, white eggs with leathery casings. Within a fortnight the same females may return again to lay another clutch. Several nests are dug and filled with eggs between early May and late August.

When the hatchlings emerge from the eggs, they dig their way out of the nest, usually in a united effort, and begin to make their way down to the sea. Researchers believe the trip down the beach to the sea is important in imprinting information the turtle needs to find its way in the sea or back to the beach where it was born. Those who become disoriented and cannot find their way to the sea, will die.

All turtles are protected by law.

Armadillos

It's believed that the first armadillos, which originated in South America, were imported into Florida from the West about 1920. The armadillo is a mammal with a hoglike snout and an armor-plated body. The armor plating isn't a rigid shell, but is made up of nine overlapping bands which move separately, allowing the shell to be flexible. The animal has a long, whiplike tail. Armadillos like to live in brushy vegetation into which they burrow. Sometimes they burrow into fields and lawns, but they don't cause any other harm, and their main diet is insects. They don't move very fast, and when they try to cross a road, they're liable to be hit by a car.

Manatees

Manatees are ponderous sea mammals, gentle creatures with a blunt snout, short front flippers, and a flat tail. They can grow to 13 feet long and weigh as much as 3,500 pounds. They're strictly vegetarian, performing a needed service by eating between 60 and 100 pounds of aquatic plants every day. Unchecked, these plants would choke a body of water. Their ancestors lived 60 million years ago in the Eocene period, but in the waters around Florida their numbers have diminished to an estimated 1,200.

Manatees, like whales, have to surface to breathe. They live in the open sea until the water becomes too cold. Then they usually seek a river and swim upstream until they find water warm enough. The warm springs of Florida are ideal for them. Convenient places to observe them from November to March are the state park at Blue Spring on the St. Johns River and at Homosassa Springs.

Manatees are dying out, not because of any commercial reasons, but because they're cut by the propellers of careless boatmen or injured by fishhooks and lines among the plants they eat. In 1988 there were 400,000 licensed boats in Florida's waters to threaten them. Harm is also done through the loss of their nesting sites, which are being taken over by people for other purposes. Still other dangers come from cold, pollution, and accidents at power plants, where the warm water tempts them to settle for the winter.

Having been protected by law since 1907, the manatees could have increased their numbers except for accidents and the hostile environment. It takes three years to rear one baby manatee: 13 months of gestation and two years of nursing. It takes minutes to kill one. If you ride a boat, remember the bumper sticker that says "I slow for manatees" is serious business. In fact, official low-speed zones in manatee territory have been established by state law.

There are three primary centers that care for sick and wounded marine life. They're Sea World, Miami Sequarium, and Homosassa Springs.

Horses and dogs

The modern horse was introduced to Florida by Hernando DeSoto, who brought 225 fine Spanish horses with him in the sixteenth century. They adapted well to the moderate climate, and until the last half of the nineteenth century, horses were the principal means of transportation.

In 1932 the legislature approved pari-mutuel wagering, and the breeding of horses in Florida picked up dramatically until today the state is third highest in the number of thoroughbreds raised in the United States. Ocala, in Marion County, is home to the Florida Thoroughbred Breeders Association, where the gentle, rolling ground is pasture for the beautiful horses. In 1985, according to the Florida Thoroughbred Breeders Association, there were 20,500 thoroughbreds in the state.

Growing in popularity are Arabian horses. Shows sponsored by the Ocala Arabian Breeders are attended by buyers and open to the public, and they have opened an attraction called the Arabian Hall of Fame.

In 1986 in Osceola County, where the headquarters for quarter horse breeders is located, voters approved racing the animals, although critics said such races wouldn't be popular. The Quarter Horse Association reports there are 47,000 of the animals in the state. Their owners are fiercely loyal. Quarter horses are sprinters, whereas thoroughbreds are better at long distance races. A quarter horse is preferred in the Western U.S. by men herding cattle; a thoroughbred is more at home on the race courses of the affluent East.

Gator Downs, in Pompano Park, offers some quarter horse racing. The other pari-mutuel tracks are Calder and Tropical Park in Miami, Florida Downs near Tampa, Gulfstream Park in Hallandale, and Hialeah Park. Pari-mutuel betting is also available at two harness tracks, ten jai-alai frontons, and eighteen greyhound tracks.

Cattle

Kissimmee (Kiss-SIM-mee) is the home of the Silver Spurs Rodeo held in February, a reminder that beef cattle is an important agricultural product of Florida. In all regions except the southern vegetable areas you'll find both beef and dairy cattle grazing in the fields. White humpbacked Brahma cattle are found side by side with domestic ones. Because of their tolerance for heat, they're used for crossbreeding. A choice mixed breed has been named the Brahmangus. In most places you will look in vain for a barn. Often cattle and horses stay outdoors year-round. When there aren't enough grasses for browsing, food troughs are set up in the fields.

Special mammals

The elusive and beautiful Florida panther, chosen by elementary school children to be the state animal, is nearly extinct. No one knows how many are still in their natural habitat, but the figure usually quoted is 30. Panthers need a large hunting area to survive—perhaps 50 square miles—and the available habitat is shrinking. The panther's story is told eloquently by a Vietnam veteran who so empathized with the animal, his words seem to come from the creature's psyche. The powerful book is *Cry of the Panther*, by James P. McMullen.

Animals fare badly when their habitats are encroached on by man. The black bear, the crocodile, and the gopher tortoise, among the larger animals, suffer from diminishing numbers. But there are many less visible living under the threat of extinction. In fact, according to biologists at the Wildlife Research Laboratory in Gainesville, there are more endangered species in Florida than anywhere else in the mainland of the United States.

The Everglades deer and the Key deer, both small ruminants, have barely escaped annihilation. A small number of Key deer survive in protected areas such as the preserve on Big Pine Key. The Everglades deer is in a no-win situation. It has trouble finding food when there's a drought and even more trouble when there's a flood. Whenever the low-lying farmlands of South Florida are threatened with too much water, pressure is on the water management district to divert the excess onto the home range of the deer, burying the grasses used as food.

One animal has prospered well: the raccoon. Its numbers have increased with the decline of predators, so that it's entirely possible that you'll encounter one. They're often friendly and come begging for food, but be careful, for an occasional raccoon is rabid.

Altogether there are 80 native species of mammals. Of the most common, those not mentioned before include mice, gophers, rats, rabbits, squirrels, opossums, and bobcats.

Fish

Shellfish

Shrimp and Florida oysters and conchs are all in diminishing supply. Even empty shells worth collecting are disappearing. Sanibel and Captiva Islands in the Gulf of Mexico just south of Fort Myers are considered among the top shelling beaches of the world. You can still pick up scallops, sand dollars, cockles, whelks, and periwinkle shells at low tide, but commercial shellers will beat you to the exotics. Some accusations have been made that people take shells which still have living creatures inside, and that, of course, would curtail the numbers of the next generation, besides being illegal in localities such as Sanibel.

Shellfish are primarily found in the pelagic areas of the sea, those on shallower shelves close to the shore. This portion is vulnerable to more local pollution, although it isn't spared the oil slicks and garbage that come from deeper waters. On the beaches, which are defined as the land between the low tide line and the dunes, there is too much churning and too much salt to

Searching for shells on Captiva Island.

support life, but where the tides don't usually reach there are salt-tolerant plants, burrowing crabs, insects, and plenty of birds.

The mangrove forests in protected areas at the edge of the sea are the cradle in which shellfish thrive. The forests are found along the coasts of peninsular Florida from Cape Canaveral south, through Florida Bay, and up the Gulf of Mexico to Cedar Key. Around the Ten Thousand Islands they are at their most luxuriant. Mangrove trees come in several varieties, but each sends out prop roots which intertwine to make a thicket of protective vegetation. The leaves and seed pods that fall into the tangle of roots attract microorganisms that use them for food. This begins the food chain that nourishes the young of marine life that shelter among the roots. Shrimp and crabs and fish grow in this natural nursery, safe from predators in the open sea. When they leave, some fall prey to the birds on the next step of the chain, but enough survive to carry on the species.

Gamefish

Among the most familiar names in saltwater fishing are these varieties: tarpon, sailfish, tuna, bonito, cobia, grouper, snapper, sea trout, flounder, mackerel, bluefish, mullet, pompano, and sheepshead. Charter boats put out from ports for those who want to pursue this exciting sport.

In lakes the largemouth bass is king of the gamefish. Its fillets are white and sweet and best eaten at once. The easiest time to catch them is in the spring (late February and early March) during spawning season when the females are ravenous and the males are busy building "nests" in the vegetation near the shoreline. Also available in freshwater lakes are pickerel, bream, perch, bluegills, crappie, and catfish. Altogether, there are 200 native varieties of freshwater fish.

Birds

Common birds

Florida is that unusual place where natives herald the arrival of the first robin of *winter.* They don't make the fuss about robins the Northerners do, even though they host the birds from November to April. The robins aren't quite the same, either. They go through an unsociable phase, and they wear their dull coats in the South.

Four hundred and twenty-five species, or half of all birds in the United States, are found in Florida. All birds are protected by law. Besides the robin, you may recognize other birds common in your old home state: sparrow, grackle, cardinal, towhee, blue jay, mockingbird, mourning dove, crow, red-winged blackbird, oriole, and meadowlark. One variety you didn't find at home is the cattle heron, a white bird properly called the cattle egret. It's about the size of a gull, with a long neck and legs and a penchant for walking along newly turned furrows or following cows in a pasture, gobbling up the insects they disturb.

When the purple martin visits Florida, he likes to take up quarters in the apartment-style birdhouses he prefers everywhere. His charming chirp is heard from February to July. The migratory martin does his bit to clean up the mosquito population as thanks for his temporary home.

So many birds migrate to, and so many pass through the state that all four classifications made by ornithologists are found here: (1) the stopovers, (2) the winter guests who return North to breed, (3) the Florida breeders, and (4) the passersby on their way to Central or South America.

Water birds

Along the shores you will find the ubiquitous gulls and terns, as well as that road-runner of the beach, the sandpiper. When they aren't fishing, the cormorants and the brown pelicans rest on pilings near the waterline. The pelicans look so ungainly on their perches, one cannot believe they're the same birds that look so lovely in flight.

Numerous long-billed birds, such as the plovers, probe the mud flats in search of crustaceans and worms to fill their bellies. The wading birds are the larger, long-legged creatures that frequent ponds and backwaters. Most notable are the great egret, the great blue heron, and the white ibis.

The great blue heron may stand some four feet tall. He has smoke blue feathers and a long neck. The great egret resembles the blue heron, but its plumage is pure white. There's also a smaller species called the snowy egret that has plumed feathers on its head, wings, and tail during breeding season. The long, curved necks of these birds are great for fishing, but when the birds are in flight, they're flexible enough to be drawn in against wind resistance.

Still another fisherman on the lakes is the osprey, often called "fish hawk." Ospreys build big permanent nests high in trees or on telegraph poles.

The flamingo, a bent-billed, pink-winged specimen, is found in collections on exhibition. Don't look for it in the wild, except for an occasional escapee. It weaves its bill through the muck at the bottom of a lake, scooping up its dinner of plants and crustaceans. Two other wading birds are close to extinction: the roseate spoonbill and the wood stork. The wood stork is a large white bird with a black head. The story of its near-extinction is typical. In 1960 birdwatchers counted 10,000 breeding pairs; in 1972 the numbers had been reduced to 3,700. The depopulation was the result of the preemption of its feeding grounds. A wood stork nests in swamps and travels as much as 50 miles a day in search of food. It has a strange method of fishing. It stirs up the shallow waters with its feet, causing small fish to come gasping to the surface for air, where it promptly eats them. The curved-bill ibis, both the white and the brown and green glossy, is another endangered wading bird.

Also on the list of water birds must be included the many varieties of ducks and coots. They don't fly and they don't fish, but they float gracefully and decoratively across the many ponds and lakes of the state, finding delicacies to eat in the growing things on the bottom of their watery milieu.

Raptors

The bald eagle builds his nest in trees, and once these have been built, the law forbids anyone to disturb the support. The ruling sometimes drives developers mad, and once in a while concessions have to be made. But how great it is to see this magnificent bird soaring high in the blue Florida sky, flashing white head and tail. Even the nest is magnificent, a huge construction of sticks and twigs, used and added to year after year.

There are many varieties of hawks in the skies, too, including the sometimes abundant red-tailed hawk and red-shouldered hawk and some species of falcons. They ride the updrafts, bank their wide wings, and swoop down on scurrying prey in the stubble of the fields. Owls are plentiful and do their share in keeping down the rodent population. Not quite in the predator class are the scavengers, notably the turkey vulture and the black vulture found throughout the state, accomplishing their ghoulish contribution in the food chain.

Insects

They crawl, they dig, they hop, they fly, they bite, they bother, they sting, they destroy, and they carry disease. It's hard to love a bug. Yet they pollinate our crops; they feed the birds, the fish, and the amphibians; they weave silk; they aerate soil; they help break down decaying things; and they make honey. They're part of nature's food chain, and they're living things in our world. We have to accept them. True Floridians acclimate themselves to sharing their space with the insects, whatever phase of their metamorphosis they're in.

The strange and the more populous insects need some introduction. A few of them are described below.

Lovebugs (*Plecia neartica*)

Lovebugs won't bite you nor contaminate your food nor spread disease nor eat your plants. They'll dirty your car and perhaps annoy you, but in a short time they'll go away to estivate or hibernate or to wherever their genes direct them. They come twice a year, in May and again in September. Each time they stay three to four weeks. Recently their numbers have been curtailed, thanks, it's believed, to the two heavy frosts that damaged the state's citrus.

They're euphemistically named because they copulate continuously while they fly. They're small, fragile bugs with lacy wings. The female flies forward, and the smaller male flies backward while the two are attached together. So engaged are they in their lovemaking that they don't fly away when you threaten them, and just swinging your hand through the air without touching them can batter them to the ground. It's a true case of love-blindness. Before 1945 there were no lovebugs in Florida, but in that year they crossed the border from Louisiana and have since progressed to cover the state.

About that car that needs protection. Lovebugs assert their right to die by self-immolation on a moving vehicle. You'll want to invest in a bug screen that can be put on and taken off the radiator portion of your car. Better still, get one coupled with a plastic deflector that can help protect your windshield. And when you get where you're going, wash the squashed bugs off with soap and water. If you've sprayed the exposed parts with a cooking spray or spread a film of kitchen oil on them, the bugs will be easier to wash off. If you don't get them off quickly, they'll pit the paint or etch the glass.

Cockroaches

The cockroach is not a pretty critter, and it doesn't make it any less repulsive to call it, as many natives do, the "palmetto bug." It can be a sizable specimen up two inches, big enough to create panic in the individual who opens a drawer suddenly and finds it there waving its antennae. It has plenty of relatives up North, and in fact, everywhere in the world. In Florida it comes in 56 varieties.

Don't let it intimidate you. You can fight back. Your first weapon of defense is to deprive it of food. Don't leave anything edible where it will be accessible. Clean even small scraps of food out of sink strainers and off the floors. Put all your bulk foods in molded plastic, metal, or glass containers, sealed tight. A cockroach will eat right through plastic bags and aluminium foil.

They like the dark, and if you turn a light on suddenly in the kitchen or bathroom at night, you'll know whether you have an infestation of the critters. If you leave your car windows open, you may surprise one in the glove compartment. They could be hiding in your boat or recreation vehicle as well. Buy inexpensive boric acid tablets in a local store and put them in shelves, drawers, and closets.

If you have an occasional roach, you can safely ignore it, but a serious infestation calls for more drastic measures. You'll have to hire someone to spray your house or do it yourself. The spray is laid down along the perimeter walls and the front edges of built-in cupboards where the traffic of the pests will spread the poison. Be sure to open the windows and turn on any fans when the job is done. You can get sick from the fumes. Many people wear a mask or a damp cloth over their noses while they spray. Remember, your pet can also be harmed by the residue on the floors.

Don't spray more often than necessary. The commercial exterminators recommend once a month, but that's overkill. It's better to wait until you see the need again.

Fire ants

You've heard ants described as "social insects," and while that may be a scientific description, "antisocial" is a more apt word for the behavior of fire ants.

They look just like the tiny ants you're familiar with. They make characteristic nests that you'll soon learn to recognize. These are made in sand and are piled up in domes wherever the terrain allows. They're everywhere, even in the cracks between slabs of concrete walks.

A fire ant is so tiny it can crawl up your legs without your being aware and bite you anywhere on your body. You won't even feel the bite at the time, but you'll know about it shortly. The area will swell and turn pink and blister, and it will smart. Just as with bee stings, some individuals may be so allergic to ant bites that they must carry an antitoxin with them at all times.

At least nine Southern states are hosts to fire ants. There are several species, according to entomologists, but they all look alike to the layman. The distinctions are only in the intensity of their bite. The ones imported from South America between 1933 and 1940 are worse than those native to Florida.

There are insecticides and baits that can be used against them, but most are more dangerous than the ants. However, it's very discouraging to a colony forming in your garden if you pour scalding water onto the incipient mound. You can keep ants away from your immediate neighborhood, but you can't eradicate them. They infest more than 30 million acres of the state. Cattle and horses in the fields suffer greatly from their bites. Take precautions when you're walking in a field or along a highway. At the least wear shoes with enclosed toes. And don't kick any sandpiles.

Termites

No state among the fifty is free of termites, but Florida is one of the most heavily infested states. And that in a world in which, entomologists say, there are more than a ton of termites for each human being. Alongside of the native termites, there is now a supertermite from Formosa (Korea). Introduced to Hawaii and then to South Carolina and Texas, it made its way to Florida in 1980 in the southeast counties of Dade and Broward.

Native termites are bad enough. They live in the wainscoting and crawl spaces chomping away at wood. Their period of activity is the springtime. After their depredations on wood, they have to return to moist soil, where they're subject to measures of control.

The common swarming termites have four wings, all of the same size and shape. They have specialized adaptations: breeders, soldiers, and workers. They usually feed on wood products. The imported ones are yellowish brown, half an inch in length, and they fly in swarms to mate. They're voracious and omnivorous. They don't require a subterranean respite; they're not affected by pesticides; they're very fast breeders; they even eat concrete.

You can check for their presence by striking wood with a hammer to see whether it's solid, or you can have the house inspected. Professionals will have to do the job of eradicating them.

Mole crickets

Mole crickets are among the most versatile critters you'll ever encounter. They can dig tunnels, walk the earth, fly, and swim. They look somewhat like brown grasshoppers an inch and a half long, but you rarely see them. They prefer to stay underground, feasting on your carefully cultivated grass.

There are three varieties of mole crickets imported from Argentina and one milder native form. Swarms of them can demolish your lawn. There are temporary and not too effective chemical controls. The most common of these for a homeowner is mole cricket bait. Put this around the infested areas, and when night falls and the crickets emerge from their tunnels, they will hopefully munch on your bait and succumb. When they're above ground they're also vulnerable to insect eaters of all kinds. They've even been known to do mankind a favor and eat each other.

Chinch bugs

When you see yellow and brown patches in your otherwise beautiful, green St. Augustine grass, one of the prime suspects should be the ½-inch long chinch bug, who is addicted to drinking the juices from the grass blades. In spite of having a long string of changes in life form (egg, five moltings of nymph, and finally adult), the chinch bug still manages three and a half generations a year. Perhaps the best solution is to plant a different type of grass or choose a native ground cover.

Nematodes

Nematodes are the ultimate in pests—they're virtually invisible. They're threadlike worms with translucent bodies, and they live underground. If plants or grass are doing poorly and there isn't an apparent explanation, pull up a root and look for galls anywhere from pinhead size to an inch in diameter. That's a sign they're probably the culprits. Dig up a portion of turf and take it to the agricultural agent in your county for verification. He may be able to give you up-to-date information on controls.

Nematodes, found throughout the United States, are difficult to eradicate. Nematocides are dangerous and difficult to apply. One method of biological control that has had promise of success is an application of commercially ground crab and shrimp shells. For a while your garden won't smell like a rose, but the bacteria growing in the decaying shells like to eat the tiny worms.

Mosquitoes

There are five dozen species of mosquitoes in Florida. It doesn't do much good to spray for them; even the trucks that come around once a week in urban areas to spray their noxious fumes on the night air don't eliminate them. You'll just have to spray *yourself* with bug repellent. If your skin is too sensitive to the chemicals, cover as much of your body as you can with clothing. A good idea is to stay indoors or behind screens during the hours of dusk when the troops are out in full force.

Three things you can do outdoors to help. First, of course, is getting rid of standing water in which the insects lay their eggs. Second is to encourage toads, lizards, and birds to share your property. You can put up birdhouses for martins and for other species of insectivorous birds. If you just put out a bird bath and keep the water clean and fresh, the birds will pay you with their protection. They can make a remarkable difference in the mosquito population. Third, you can fight back with a blue-light bug trap. You'll be gratified by the buzzing sound that means another mosquito has been zapped, but it's only a skirmish and not a winning battle. Besides, it could be a friendly bug that just died.

One predatory insect that likes to eat mosquitoes is the mud dauber wasp. Because wasps have a reputation for stinging, most folks are afraid of this harmless member of the family. Sometimes erroneously called paper wasps, the mud dauber is about an inch and a half long, brown, and buzzless. It can be recognized by the nests it builds in protected places like eaves and the ceilings of porches. The nests are gray and papery with hexagonal cells. Unless they're blocking your drainpipes or the outlet from your cooking fan, let them stay where they are.

Other critters

Gnats, sandflies, fleas, chiggers, and a tiny creature with the descriptive name of "no-seeums" are pests that nip tender flesh and like to fly into ears and hair, places where people can't put protective repellents. Chiggers nest in Spanish moss. Ticks lurk among the grasses and the wetlands. A larger insect, the deer fly, which looks like a blond housefly, has a particularly nasty bite. They swarm about in the dusk of evening. It's a good idea to leave the battlefield to them for their few hours.

The Mediterranean fruit fly won't attack people, but it loves to burrow into citrus fruit. A Med fly has four metamorphoses—egg, larva, pupa, adult—through which it passes in anywhere from 17 to 25 days, depending on the weather. You can readily see how many generations a year that makes possible.

Scorpions are big arachnids, from three to five inches long. They aren't often found near "civilization." The well-publicized variety has a poison gland that sends its victims for emergency treatment to the nearest doctor or hospital. A less well-known variety, called the whip scorpion, performs a sterling service free to humanity: it eats cockroaches. You can recognize this species by its whiplike tail, which easily distinguishes it from the poisonous one with a segmented tail.

Whiteflies and caterpillars, sod webworms, earwigs, silverfish, and the like, which make their homes up North, have relatives living in Florida. Besides these, there's also a prospective invasion of killer bees. Only the infamous Japanese beetle, whose midsummer depredations are common in the Eastern United States, doesn't feel at home in Florida.

Fighting back

Don't give up. There are some weapons in your arsenal. Organic fertilizers and biological controls and common sense are on your side. Try these suggestions:

Encourage insectivorous birds.   Among the best of these are the purple martins who will repay you for the nesting house you provide them by eating many times their weight in mosquitoes.

Don't tell lady bugs to "fly away home."   If you don't see these little beetles with black dots on their red shells, order a supply from a nurseryman or seed catalog. Their favorite meal is aphids.

Be kind to toads, frogs, and spiders.   They're world-class catchers of flying pests.

Cultivate marigolds.   There's something about them that insects don't like. In fact, it's hard to find a diseased marigold. Their presence discourages even soil-dwelling pests like nematodes. Some people scatter camphor balls about or plant garlic to discourage crawling insects.

Grow healthy plants.   Use organic materials to keep the ground friable and to feed the plants. They're effective and are harmless to the environment. Learn to be an expert composter. Healthy plants are likely to survive run-of-the-mill assaults by pests. Besides feeding them well, give them good root protection and conserve moisture by mulching.

Use safe controls.   Minimize and if possible eliminate the use of chemical sprays. Dust with sulfur for leaf mold and fungus. Use a weak solution of bleach for aphid infestations, which you can apply by hand to individual plants. Lay down specific baits.

Raise your level of tolerance for bugs.   Not all of them are harmful. If humans poison the ground with insecticides, they upset the balance of nature. The poisons get into the food chain: they kill the birds and fish; they pass through the bloodstreams of animals to contaminate dairy products, meat, and eggs; they coat the fruits we grow.

If you're discouraged by the many flaws in paradise, you're all ready to have your spirits raised. May you find hope for the remainder of your life in the last chapter of this book.

13. The Good Life

It's one of those memorable moments of your lifetime when you cross the border of Florida to your find your new home.

It's a little frightening to make such a major commitment. You worked hard; you raised your children; you shared your life with friends; you joined organizations; you had the security of relatives around you. The ties that bound you were strong, and you've broken them. No wonder you're concerned about whether you made the right move.

When you were just a tourist, you paid your money and had a good time. If the weather or the fishing weren't good, you could always go back home. If the traffic was heavy, you could blame it on the tourist season. If the prices were steep you could say it was resort taxes or the usual tariff for seasonal services. You could relax in your comfortable room and not worry about damage from high winds and pollution and insect control and legal matters. Now they're going to be *your* problems.

Don't worry. This can be the best time of your life. There are many new things to learn and to relish. There are leisure days and nights, a fine climate, and places to explore that you never visited before. You can say good-bye to thermal underwear, heavy coats and slacks, galoshes, scarves, and woolen caps. You can relegate the snowshovel to a distant memory.

There will be new supermarkets and shopping malls to discover and local banks to handle your money. A new church will welcome you and so will many of the clubs you knew back home. You'll find a doctor, a well-staffed hospital, and a car repair shop. All the services and conveniences that are endemic to America are here. And, in addition, there are all the exciting attractions to visit. And the super deals for resident senior citizens.

Before long the summers won't seem too hot, and the thundershowers will be welcome. You'll look forward to the uncrowded roads and parking lots of the off-season. The stiff lawn grasses won't look like crabgrass any more. You'll love the convenience of casual clothes. An alligator in the lake will no longer be a novelty, and palm trees will be ho-hum. Even the bugs will be only a minor inconvenience.

You'll rejoice in the seasons. Spring is early strawberries and fresh leaves on the trees, and put-away-the-sweater time. Summer is cool breezes off the ocean and lush greens jeweled with raindrops. Fall is warmth and clear blue skies and a flash of color from the sweetgums and maples. Winter is cool, sometimes nippy but never biting, and its skies are full of flocking birds.

Of course, you can't escape the reminders of getting older; they go with retirement. But you won't get winter colds in Florida, and the easier life won't tax your heart as much. The warmth will be kinder to stiffening joints, and outdoor activities may help to discourage the "spare tire" from growing around your midriff. And hopefully you'll be able to enjoy these pleasures for a long time. Just think, if you retire here at 62, before you're 70, you'll have spent a tenth of your life in retirement!

The best thing of all in the Good Life can be new friends. If you make your home in an "adult" park or condominium or apartment house or subdivision, you'll be surrounded by people just like you. They are the kind of citizens a community loves: law abiding, concerned, and contributing. They're easy to meet at the clubs, the links, the pools, the game rooms, and the potluck dinners.

Before long you'll be forging friendships, the kind that are close enough and trusting enough to call on one another at the last minute for an evening out. A relationship in which each is ready to lend the traditional cup of sugar without ever remembering it was borrowed. One in which you both know the names of each other's grandchildren. The kind of friends that you can call on in an emergency, or who help you through periods of unhappiness. In short, a new family.

Welcome to Florida. Happy retirement, and have a good life.

If anybody asks what you're doing, just say you're "out," having a good life in Florida.

H. Milo Stewart III

APPENDICES

I. STATE AND NATIONAL PARKS

FLORIDA'S STATE PARKS

This material is provided by the Department of Natural Resources, Division of Recreation and Parks. For more information, write to the Department at 3900 Commonwealth Blvd., Tallahassee, Fl 32399. The code letters below indicate the type of facility and the symbols indicate the availability of camping sites:

A ....Archaeological Site
B ....Botanical Site
G ....Geological Site
H ....Historical Site
M ....Museum
OG ....Ornamental Gardens
P ....Park
PS ....Nature Preserve
RA ....Recreational Area
RS ....Reserve
* tent and trailer camping
# vacation cabins

RA* Anastasia, St. Augustine Beach, off SR A1A
RA* Bahia Honda, Bahia Honda Key, off US 1
H   Barnacle, The, Coconut Grove, Main Highway
RA   Big Lagoon, 10 mi. SW of Pensacola, off SR 292
P*   Blackwater River, 15 mi. NE of Milton, off US 90
P*   Blue Spring, 2 mi. W of Orange City, off I-4 & SR 17
P   Bulow Creek, N of Ormond Beach
H   Bulow Plantation Ruins, SE of Bunnell, off SR S5A
P   Caladesi Island, offshore Dunedin, from US 19A
RA   Cape Florida, Bill Baggs, Key Biscayne, off US 1
PS   Cape St. George, offshore of Apalachicola
P   Cayo Costa, offshore Boca Grande, accessible by boat
M,H Cedar Key, Cedar Key off SR 24
RA* Chekika, 11 mi. NW of Homestead

P*   Collier-Seminole, 17 mi. S of Naples
M   Constitutional Convention, Port St. Joe, off US 98
A   Crystal River, NW of Crystal River off US 19-98
H   Dade Battlefield, Bushnell, off US 301
RA*   Dead Lakes, 4 mi. N of Wewahitchka off SR 71
RA   DeLeon Springs, DeLeon Springs, off US 17
RA   Delnor-Wiggins Pass, 6 mi. S of Bonita Springs
G   Devil's Millhopper, 2 mi. NW of Gainesville
RA   Don Pedro Island, offshore of Placida, access by boat
OG   Eden, Point Washington, off US 98
PS   Fakahatchee Strand, 16 mi. E of Collier-Seminole
         (above)
RA*   Falling Waters, 3 mi. S of Chipley, off SR 77A
P*   Faver-Dykes, 15 mi. S of St. Augustine
RA*   Flagler Beach, Flagler Beach, off SR A1A
P*   Florida Caverns, 3 mi. N of Marianna, off SR 167
M   Forest Capital, S of Perry, off US 98-27A
P*   Fort Clinch, Fernandina Beach, off SR A1A
P   Fort Cooper, Inverness, off Old Floral City Road
H   Fort Gadsden, 6 mi. SW of Sumatra, off SR 65
RA   Fort Pierce Inlet, 4 mi. E of Ft. Pierce
H   Fort Zachary Taylor, Key West
H   Gamble Plantation, Ellenton, off US 301
RA   Gasparilla Island, S of Placida on CR 775
P*#   Gold Head Branch, Mike Roess, 6 mi. NE of
         Keystone Hts.
RA*   Grayton Beach, Grayton Beach, off SR 30AS
RA   Henderson Beach, Destin, on US 98W
P*   Highlands Hammock, 6 mi. W of Sebring
P*   Hillsborough River, 6 mi. SW of Zephyrhills
RA   Honeymoon Island, Dunedin, SR 586
P*   Hontoon Island, 16 mi. W of DeLand, off SR 44
RA   Hugh Taylor Birch, Ft. Lauderdale, off SR A1A
P   Ichetucknee Springs, 4 mi. NW of Fort White
H   Indian Key, near Islamorada, accessible by boat
P   John D. MacArthur Beach, N. Palm Beach on
         Singer Is.
M   John Gorrie, Apalachicola, off US 319-98
RA   John U. Lloyd Beach, Dania, off SR A1A
P*   John Pennekamp Coral Reef, Key Largo
P*#   Jonathan Dickinson, 13 mi. S of Stuart
H   Kingsley Plantation, Fort George, off SR A1A

H	Koreshan, Estero, off US41
RA*	Lake Griffin, Fruitland Park, off US 27-441
RA	Lake Jackson Mounds, 2 mi. N of I-10, Tallahassee
P	Lake Kissimmee, 15 mi. E of Lake Wales
P	Lake Louisa, 7 mi. SW of Clermont
RA	Lake Manatee, 14 mi. E of Bradenton, off SR 64
RA	Lake Talquin, 20 mi. W of Tallahasse, off SR 20
B	Lignumvitae Key, off Lower Matecumbe, accessible by boat
RA	Little Manatee River, 4 mi. S of Sun City
P*	Little Talbot Island, 17 mi. NE of Jacksonville
RA*	Long Key, Long Key
OG	Maclay, Alfred B., Tallahassee, off US 319
A	Madira Bickel Mound, Terra Ceia Is., off US 19
P*	Manatee Springs, 6 mi. W of Chiefland, off SR 320
H	Marjorie Kinnan Rawlings, Cross Creek
P*#	Myakka River, 17 mi. E of Sarasota, off SR 72
H	Natural Bridge Battlefield, 6 mi. E of Woodville
H	New Smyrna Sugar Mills Ruins, New Smyrna Beach
P*	Ochlockonee River, 4 mi. S of Sopchoppy
P*	O'leno, 20 mi. S of Lake City, off US 41
RA	Oleta River, N. Miami, off US 1
H	Olustee Battlefield, 2 mi. E of Olustee, off US 90
RA*	Oscar Scherer, 2 mi. S of Osprey, off US 41
H	Paynes Creek, ½ mi. E of Bowling Green
PS	Paynes Prairie, Micanopy, off US 441
RA	Perdido Key, 15 mi. SW of Pensacola, off SR 292
RA	Ponce DeLeon Springs, off US 90 on SR 181A
PS	Prairie-Lakes, Kenansville, W on SR 523 from US 441
OG	Ravine, Palatka, off Twigg St.
RS	Rock Springs Run, Sorrento, SR 46
RA*	Rocky Bayou, Fred Gannon, 5 mi. N of Niceville
RA*	St. Andrews, 3 mi. E of Panama City Beach, off SR 392
P*	St. George Island, 10 mi. SE of Eastpoint, off US 98
P*#	St. Joseph Peninsula, near Port St. Joe, off CR 30
RA	St. Lucie Inlet, Port Salerno, accessible by boat
PS	San Felasco Hammock, 4 mi. NW of Gainesville
H	San Marcos de Apalache, St. Marks, off SR 363
RA*	Sebastian Inlet, Sebastian Inlet, SR A1A
H	Stephen Foster Folk Center, White Springs, off US 41
P*	Suwannee River, 13 mi. W of Live Oak, off US 90

RS   Tenoroc, NE of Lakeland, on SR 33A
RA*   Three Rivers, 1 mi. N of Sneads, off SR 271
P*   Tomoka, 3 mi. N of Ormond Beach
P*   Torreya, between Bristol & Greensboro
RS   Tosohatchee, S of Christmas
PS   Waccasassa Bay, E of Cedar Key, SR 24
P   Wakulla Springs, Edward Ball, Wakulla Springs
OG   Washington Oaks, 3 mi. S of Marineland
RA   Weedon Island, St. Petersburg, S of US 92
P   Wekiwa Springs, N of Orlando, E of Apopka
H   Ybor City, Tampa, exit 21 off I-4
H   Yulee Sugar Mill Ruins, Old Homosassa, off SR 490

Key: * tent and trailer camping
        # vacation cabins

STATE FORESTS

*   Blackwater River
      Cary
*   Pine Log
*   Withlacoochee

U.S. PARKS AND FOREST SERVICES

*   Appalachicola National Forest
*   Big Cypress National Preserve
*   Biscayne National Park
      Castillo de San Marcos National Memorial
      DeSoto National Monument
*#   Everglades National Park
      Fort Caroline National Memorial
*   Fort Jefferson National Monument
      Fort Matanzas National Monument
*#   Gulf Islands National Seashore
*   Ocala National Forest
*   Osceola National Forest

APPENDIX II.   COMMUNITY COLLEGES

College	City
Brevard	Cocoa
Broward	Fort Lauderdale
Central Florida	Ocala
Chipola	Marianna
Daytona Beach (Volusia)	Daytona Beach
Edison	Fort Myers
Florida Junior College	Jacksonville
Florida Keys	Key West
Gulf Coast	Panama City
Hillsborough	Tampa
Indian River	Fort Pierce
Lake City	Lake City
Lake-Sumter	Leesburg
Manatee	Bradenton
Miami-Dade	Miami
North Florida	Madison
Okaloosa-Walton	Niceville
Palm Beach	Palm Beach
Pasco-Hernando	Dade City
Pensacola	Pensacola
Polk	Winter Haven
St. Johns River	Palatka
St. Petersburg	St. Petersburg
Santa Fe	Gainesville
Seminole	Sanford
South Florida	Avon Park
Tallahassee	Tallahassee
Valencia	Orlando

APPENDIX III.   FLORIDA'S MAJOR SPRINGS

Spring	Nearest City	Mil.Gal./Day
Spring Creek	Tallahassee	1,294
Crystal River	Crystal River	592
Silver	Ocala	529
Rainbow	Dunellon	493
Alapha Rise	Live Oak	392
St. Marks	Tallahassee	335
Wakulla	Tallahassee	252
Wacissa Group	Wacissa	251
Ichetucknee	Fort White	233
Holton	Hamilton County (access by boat)	186
Blue Springs	Marianna	122
Manatee	Chiefland	116
Weeki Wachee	Brooksville	113
Kini	Tallahassee	113
Homosassa	Homosassa	113
Troy	Branford	107
Hornsby	High Springs	105
Blue Spring	Orange City	104
Gainer	Bennett	102
Falmouth	Live Oak	102
Chassahowitzka	Homosassa	89
Alexander	Ocala Forest	77
Blue Spring	Madison	74
Silver Glen	Astor	72
Natural Bridge	Woodville	68
Fanning Springs	Fanning Springs	72

(Sources: U.S. Geological Survey, and
Florida Department of Natural Resources)

APPENDIX IV.   COUNTIES AND COUNTY SEATS

Alachua, Gainesville
Baker, Macclenny
Bay, Panama City
Bradford, Starke
Brevard, Titusville
Broward, Fort Lauderdale
Calhoun, Blountstown
Charlotte, Punta Gorda
Citrus, Inverness
Clay, Green Cove Springs
Collier, East Naples
Columbia, Lake City
Dade, Miami
DeSoto, Arcadia
Dixie, Cross City
Duval, Jacksonville
Escambia, Pensacola
Flagler, Bunnell
Franklin, Apalachicola
Gadsden, Quincy
Gilchrist, Trenton
Glades, Moore Haven
Gulf, Port St. Joe
Hamilton, Jasper
Hardee, Wauchula
Hendry, LaBelle
Hernando, Brooksville
Highlands, Sebring
Hillsborough, Tampa
Holmes, Bonifay
Indian River, Vero Beach
Jackson, Marianna
Jefferson, Monticello
Lafayette, Mayo

Lake, Tavares
Lee, Fort Myers
Leon, Tallahassee
Levy, Bronson
Liberty, Bristol
Madison, Madison
Manatee, Bradenton
Marion, Ocala
Martin, Stuart
Monroe, Key West
Nassau, Fernandina Beach
Okaloosa, Crestview
Okeechobee, Okeechobee
Orange, Orlando
Osceola, Kissimmee
Palm Beach, W. Palm Beach
Pasco, Dade City
Pinellas, Clearwater
Polk, Bartow
Putnam, Palatka
St. Johns, St. Augustine
St. Lucie, Fort Pierce
Santa Rosa, Milton
Sarasota, Sarasota
Seminole, Sanford
Sumter, Bushnell
Suwannee, Live Oak
Taylor, Perry
Union, Lake Butler
Volusia, DeLand
Wakulla, Crawfordville
Walton, DeFuniak Springs
Washington, Chipley

APPENDIX V.   HURRICANE INFORMATION

Code No.	Description	Beaufort Scale of Wind Velocities Pressure (lb/psf)	Speed (mph)
0	Calm	0	Below 1
1	Light air	0.01	1-3
2	Light breeze	0.08	4-7
3	Gentle breeze	0.28	8-12
4	Moderate breeze	0.67	13-18
5	Fresh breeze	1.31	19-24
6	Strong breeze	2.3	25-31
7	Moderate gale	3.6	32-38
8	Fresh gale	5.4	39-46
9	Strong gale	7.7	47-54
10	Whole gale	10.5	55-63
11	Storm	14.0	64-75
12	Hurricane	Above 17	Above 75

Descriptive terms for the numbers above are:

0, smoke rises straight up
1, smoke drifts slightly
2, feel wind on face
3, flags fly straight
4, small branches move
5, waves have crests
6, large branches move

7, difficult walking
8, twigs break off
9, branches break
10, structural damage
11, much damage
12, excessive damage

Meteorological Terms

Tropical Disturbance: Winds begin circulation pattern in upper air. Unequal atmospheric pressure begins.

Tropical Depression: Winds up to 39 mph circulate near surface. Low pressure areas develop.

Tropical Storm: Marked pressure difference and wind speeds up to 74 mph.

Tropical Storm Watch: Storm may strike coast in 36 hours.

Tropical Storm Warning: Time factor is reduced to 24 hours.

Hurricane Watch: Threat of a possible hurricane striking coast in 36 hours.

Hurricane Warning: Within 24 hours or less a hurricane is expected to strike the coast.

BIBLIOGRAPHY

Babinchak, John II, ed. *Florida Forecast '88*. Orlando: Sentinel Communications Company, 1988.

Brown, Robin C. *Florida's Fossils*. Sarasota: Pineapple Press, 1988.

Brown, Virginia Pounds, and Laurella Owens. *The World of Southern Indians*. Birmingham: Beechwood Books, 1983.

Burchfill, B. Clark, et al. *Physical Geology*. Columbus: Charles E. Merrill Publishing Company, 1982.

Bush, Charles S., and Julia F. Morton. *Native Trees and Plants for Florida Landscaping*, Bulletin No. 193. Tallahassee: Florida Department of Agriculture and Consumer Services, undated.

Campbell, George. *An Illustrated Guide to Some Poisonous Plants and Animals of Florida*. Sarasota: Pineapple Press, 1983.

Carr, Archie, and Coleman J. Green. *Guide to the Reptiles, Amphibians, and Freshwater Fishes of Florida*. Gainesville: University Presses of Florida, 1955.

Copeland, Leila S., and J.E. Dovell. *La Florida, Its Land and People*. Austin: The Steck Company, 1957.

Douglas, Marjory Stoneman. *The Everglades: River of Grass*. Sarasota: Pineapple Press, 1988 (new edition) Extension Pesticide Program Committee. *Apply Pesticides Properly*. Gainesville: Institute of Food and Agricultural Sciences, University of Florida, undated.

Florida Department of Business Regulation. *Buying a Condominium* (pamphlet). Tallahassee, 1986.

Florida Department of Commerce, Division of Tourism. *Florida, (six regions),* undated.

Florida Department of Community Affairs and Miami Jewish Home and Hospital for the Aged, Inc. *Housing Solutions for Florida Seniors, a How-to Manual*. Tallahassee, undated.

Florida Department of Natural Resources, Division of Recreation and Parks. *Florida State Parks.* Tallahassee: undated.

Hubin, Vincent J. *Warning! Condominium Ownership May Be Dangerous to Your Health, Wealth, and Peace of Mind.* Homewood, Il: Dow-Jones-Irwin, 1976.

Marth, Del, and Martha J. Marth. *The Florida Almanac, 1988-89 (7th edition).* Gretna, LA: Pelican Publishing Company, 1985.

Maxwell, Lewis S. *Florida Plant Selector.* Tampa: Lewis S. Maxwell, 1961.

McMullen, James. *Cry of the Panther.* Sarasota: Pineapple Press, 1984.

Mohlenbrock, Robert. *You Can Grow Tropical Fruit Trees.* St. Petersburg: Great Outdoors Publishing Company, 1980.

Morris, Allen. *The Florida Handbook, 1985-1986.* Tallahassee: Peninsular Publishing Company, 1985.

Ocala Arabian Breeders Society. *Ocala Arabian Directory.* (brochure) 1981.

Rabkin, Richard, and Jacob Rabkin. *Nature Guide to Florida.* Miami: Banyan Books, 1978.

Shoemeyer, Anne H., ed. *Florida Statistical Abstract* (21st Edition). Gainesville: University Presses of Florida, 1987.

Smiley, Nixon. *Tropical Planting and Gardening for South Florida and the West Indies.* Coral Gables: University of Miami Press, 1960.

Tucker, James A. *Florida Birds, How to Attract, Feed and Know Them.* Tampa: Lewis S. Maxwell, 1968.

Watkins, John V., and Thomas J. Sheehan. *Florida Landscape Plants, Native and Exotic.* Gainesville: The University Presses of Florida, 1975.

Wood, Dr. Roland et al. *New Florida Atlas.* Tallahassee: Trend Publishing company, 1981.

Zak, Bill. *Florida Critters.* Dallas: Taylor Publishing Company, 1986.

INDEX